SEVEN TREASURES

MYSTERY STORIES

OMAR ZAHID

Written by: **Omar Zahid**

Creative Editors: **Bard** (AI)

Editors: **Bing** (AI)

Cover Illustration: **Neural.Love** (AI generated image), Omar Zahid

Cover Design: **Omar Zahid** (Fotor software, Neural.Love)

Book Design: **Designer 8**

Book Formatting: hmrashed

Printing Company: **Lightning Source Ltd.**, UK

International Publishing Platform: **IngramSpark**, US

Publisher: **Maxmilian Nemec - Tanezcor, CR**

Mailing Address: Tanezcor Pictures LLC, Suite 1700, 444 River Point, Chicago 60606, IL, US

Published: August 2023

ISBN: 978-80-908692-2-6

SEVEN TREASURES

The Greatest Treasure is Your Life Power
Mystery Stories

What if you could experience a variety of different lives, each one more extraordinary than the last? In this book, you will discover seven + one stories that are inspired by real events, but transformed by the power of imagination.

You will encounter:

A man who finds himself trapped on a haunted ship in the midst of a raging storm.

A psychiatrist who struggles with his own demons and decides to take a drastic step.

A child of the urban jungle who defies the odds and achieves her dreams in America.

A spaceship general who travels to Earth to deliver a vital message to a holy place.

A geologist who is hired by a wealthy gallery owner to find a precious gem in Europe and faces a deadly challenge.

A Nazi hypnotist who tests his new methods on his friend and alters his fate in a surprising way.

A king who renounces his throne and starts a new life from scratch.

And a man who is visited by the messengers of the dream realm and learns the secret of existence.

These are the treasures that you will uncover in this collection of stories. Are you ready to find out more?

The Greatest Treasure is Your Life Power

Be it darkness, be it light

The God knows already

That you'll make it through all trials despite

And Nathrengar is here for you to test

What's fun and what's not best

What's wrong and what's right

It's now or never, it's ever thus

Be it darkness, be it light

It's the seven-treasures-story night

Contents

Story 1: The Night of Power - Layalat al Quadr 1

Story 2: Mr. Pain Killer 11

Story 3: Seven Treasures 16

Story 4: Anitta 42

Story 5: Introduction to Hypnosis by
Heinrich Cristian Columbus 59

Story 6: Nathrengar's Necklace 91

Story 7: King & Bard 124

Story 8: The Gem for Princess 129

The Night of Power - Layalat al Quadr

Fatima was a young woman with a big heart and a big family. She lived in the Red City with her husband - but he was gravely ill and could not walk, let alone work, with five children and grandparents. Fatima was a kind and generous woman, but she was also very poor. She had no job or money and was struggling to support her family.

One day, Fatima was getting ready for the Night of Power. She fasted all day and spent the evening reading the Koran and praying. She was full of hope, knowing that this night could change her life.

At midnight, Fatima went to the mosque to pray. The mosque was crowded with people all seeking the rewards of the Night of Power. Fatima found a calm place in a corner and began to pray. She prayed for her family, friends and community. She prayed for peace and prosperity in the world. She prayed for guidance and forgiveness.

When Fatima prayed, she felt tranquility and joy. She felt closer to God than ever before. She knew this was a night she would always remember.

Suddenly, out of nowhere, she had a vision. She saw a good angel…

The strange, good-emitting being appeared for a brief moment in the shape of a yellow-orange cloud or phosphorescent tiger-like puff under the mosque's chandelier.

The entity was communicating with a young beautiful woman using telepathy.

The angel told Fatima that she would be helped and that she would find a way to provide for her family.

Tears of gratitude rolled down Fatima's face.

When the sun rose, Fatima left the mosque rejuvenated and inspired. She knew she had made the best of the Night of Power. She was resolved to live her life in a way that pleased God.

***

General Andromeda found himself in a kind of dark impenetrable forest, and at first he didn't even know what he was doing here, until he realised that he was holding a wicker basket in his hand.

In that basket were the mushrooms he had picked.

And then it suddenly dawned on him.

He must have either blacked out or had a sudden memory loss of dramatic proportions.

"Meow,…meow,…" came from the basket and the man noticed that there were no more mushrooms in the basket, but a cat - such a tabby from the streets of the big city.

However, the general was not surprised, he figured that this version of the universe was quite unstable.

He reached into his pocket and felt the stone.

Then he pulled it out and examined it with sharp eyes against the indigo blue light of the full moon.

It was a red diamond - raw - uncut - and yet sparkling with bloody beauty, and emitting a kind of inexplicable savage power.

"He must find a way to the Red City! He must find it tonight!"

"The imams are already eagerly waiting for him,…they urgently need the stone!"

"But how do you get there—from here—and where exactly is it? How far is it from the Red City, which is supposed to be somewhere near the desert called the Sahara?"

This is how General Andromeda thought, and thought quite hard.

The tall, skinny man suddenly turned around and pointed a flashlight in front of him.

Somewhere back in the shrubs there was a roar - a bear!

General Andromeda quickly reached into his pocket for the pepper spray…

But then there was a threatening sound that sounded more like a tiger.

And indeed, a large head with yellow-green eyes and big fangs emerged from the bushes.

This was not good.

The beast of the night crawled towards him and seemed to arch, squat - in preparation for a jump that would be fatal for General Andromeda.

He could already faintly feel how the beast's jagged, sharp teeth were tearing his jugular veins and ripping the hot innards from his body.

And the blood spatters and splashes on the leaves of the dark trees and ferns.

He took the spray out of his pocket, but *he already knew that it wouldn't help him twice.*

It was strange that the menacing animal somehow mysteriously and most unexpectedly glowed with a yellow-orange colour, while the black stripes changed their colour to blue and green and then back to black.

There was thunder in the distance.

And then something unexpected happened - the tiger turned into a mere cloud - haze - something like bluish smoke from a cigar.

And the cloud suddenly spoke to the General and introduced himself as…

…Angel Xy - and that *it will show him the way to the Red City, that he knows a shortcut - something like a wormhole - or a rabbit hole.*

Andromeda followed the mysterious entity.

They walked through a gorge, through bushes, and crossed a dark river whose current dragged the General and tested the strength of his will to survive.

Then they arrived at a clearing in the middle of the forest.

Then the entity instructed the General to take the diamond out of his pocket and place it over his heart, repeating this mantra:

I'm fast and strong like a red diamond flying in the night.
I overcome all obstacles with patience and persistence.
I am guided by the light of my faith and
I know that I will reach my destination,
the Red City.

And the man repeated this chant over and over.

Leaves and branches whirled around General Andromeda, and some fairies appeared that they danced around him in a dazzling rhythm. It was like a sudden storm, like a tornado, and he was in its eye.

Then lightning struck - right at the General, and he vanished.

***

General Andromeda stirred from his slumber in the desert, under a canopy of stars that glittered like jewels. He lifted his head and spat out a mouthful of sand. He squinted at the horizon, where a faint silhouette of the Red City loomed. It was not a mirage, he was sure of it.

He glanced at his bracelet and flicked his wrist to summon a hologram of a computer screen. He searched the web for the coordinates of his destination and confirmed that he was only 17 kilometres away from the city.

He flicked his wrist again and the hologram vanished into the golden bracelet. He gazed at the city with awe and anticipation, its ancient buildings rising from the dunes like a mirage of their own. This was the place that Allah had blessed, the place where history and mystery intertwined.

General Andromeda felt a surge of impatience, he longed to reach the city as soon as possible and explore its secrets. He wanted to walk on the cobblestones of the narrow alleys, to smell the incense of the mosque, to hear the voices of the people, to taste the flavours of the cafes, to watch the sunrise over the desert. He had been alone for too long, traveling across the endless universe from galaxy to galaxy, but this morning - this morning he would be reborn…

And so he hastened, clutching a red diamond in his hand that guided him to his destiny.

***

General Andromeda pounded on the door, but there was only silence.

He spotted that the window of the balcony was slightly open.

The man climbed the roof, scrambled up the sheer stone wall and jumped down to the balcony floor.

He sneaked down the stairs, touching the cold walls in the dark hallway.

Then he pulled out a red diamond crystal from his pocket.

He held the gem to his heart, and beams of dazzling light erupted.

Andromeda stopped at the door of the room, torn for a moment, but then he made his choice and morphed into a small cloud that shimmered with yellow and orange shades.

He floated through the door like a specter, and his identity dissolved into the emptiness of space.

His memory soared back to the central quantum computer - the singularity - at the core of the Andromeda galaxy, where it was saved in a file called "The Book of Knowledge".

***

Somewhere in a modest house on the fringe of the Red City, a boy was born and they named him Andromeda al Amin.

There were people crowded around the crib, and one of them - a mysterious stranger in a long black cloak and a black hat, whose face was shrouded by a shadow - slipped a red rough diamond into the baby's small hand.

And the people celebrated, for they had seen again the miracle of life's emergence.

They were also astonished by the generosity of that man, whom no one knew, and who, in reality, everyone knew…

He was everywhere - the lord of darkness - in everything - in birth and death and he knew everything - for such was his task - by the will of the supreme, invisible and infinitely compassionate Allah.

***

The Red City in the Sahara Desert was alive with movement. It was the Night of Power, the most sacred night of the Islamic year. Muslims from all corners of the world came to the city to pray and seek God's mercy.

In the Grand Mosque, imams guided the congregation in prayer. The choir was composed of people from all backgrounds, rich and poor, young and old. They were all united in their faith and hope for a brighter meaningful future.

Andromeda al Amin was among the congregation. He was a mighty warlord, but he was also a devout Muslim. He came to the Red City to seek God's wisdom on how to lead his people.

As General Andromeda prayed, he felt a sense of serenity and tranquility. He felt closer to God than ever before. He knew that God would show him the right way.

Suddenly Andromeda had a vision. He saw the archangel Gabriel in a vision. Gabriel held a red diamond in his hand. The diamond glowed with a radiant light.

Gabriel spoke to Andromeda. He told him that the diamond was a gift from God. He said the diamond would give Andromeda the power to see the reality.

Andromeda took the diamond from Gabriel. He held it in his hand and closed his eyes. When he opened his eyes, he saw the world in a new light. He saw that this life was just an illusion. He saw that Jannah, the Garden of Eden, was the true world.

Andromeda was filled with bliss. He knew he had received a great blessing. He was resolved to use the diamond to help others and make the world a better place.

Andromeda left the mosque and went out into the city. He began to teach the people. He told them about the vision he had seen. He told them about the red diamond and the power it has.

People were astonished by the story of Andromeda. They had never heard anything like it before. They were curious to know more about Jannah and the afterlife.

General Andromeda continued to teach for many days. He told the people about the significance of faith, prayer and love. He told them about the rewards that await them in Jannah.

People were motivated by the words of Andromeda. They began to live their lives in a more virtuous, more mindful way. They prayed more often, gave more charity, and treated each other with more compassion.

Andromeda's message spread throughout Red City. Soon people were coming from all over the world to hear him teach. He became known as a great spiritual leader and his teachings helped change the world for good.

***

As Andromeda wandered in the enchanted garden, where palms and fountains adorned the oasis near the Red City, he heard a familiar melody. It was coming from a harp, held by a lovely maiden.

He approached her and asked with curiosity, "What is your name?"

She gazed at him and replied with a tinkling voice, "You don't know me, do you? Have you lost me in your dreams?"

He felt a pang of nostalgia and said softly, "I feel like we have crossed paths before…"

She smiled and said, "I am the Bard, Andromeda,…once there was a king,…" and she strummed the harp again, as if nothing mattered…

And then she started to tell a poem of ancient times, and Andromeda joined her now and then, as golden memories flooded his mind:

You will rise once more

Don't lose hope, my friend for you will rise once more.

Allah is always by your side, so lift yourself with pride.

Allahu Akbar!

The night may seem long but the dawn will always break through.

The sorrow may be heavy, but peace will come.

Allahu Akbar!

So don't lose hope, my friend for you will rise once more.

Allah is always by your side, so lift yourself with pride.

Allahu Akbar!

Mr. Pain Killer

You soar over the endless field of sunflowers, feeling the breeze on your face. The melody of an Andalusian guitar fills your ears, soothing your soul. The sun warms your skin and you are in love, but you don't know the reason...

From the diary of Doctor Stephan Mephistopheles Ray

Friday, January 27, 2023

Writing down my dreams has always been a habit of mine. Every morning, I would update my diary with the latest details of my nocturnal adventures. Writing is more than a hobby for me - it's a passion. But it's not my profession. I'm a doctor by trade - a psychiatrist at Bradford Royal Infirmary. Right now, I'm on holiday in Andalusia, Spain - alone and loving it. I enjoy the solitude and the scenery. I moved to the UK in 2001 from a small, forgotten town in Romania. After graduating from the University of Cluj, I ran my own private practice and collaborated with the social services and police in Bucharest. I never married or had a girlfriend - at least, not a serious one. I was always a lone wolf.

The Carpathian forests are home to many creatures, both living and undead. Deadly bears and mythical vampires roam the woods, looking for prey. I loved to wander in these woods at night, alone and fearless. I felt a thrill when the full moon cast its light on the ancient trees and the rocky cracks. I was not immune to fear, but I enjoyed it. I could walk for miles and miles across the hills. I also liked to record the sounds of the forest and make them into eerie music - the kind that would make your skin crawl and your heart race. But something has changed in me lately. Something is wrong with my mind. Sometimes I find myself sitting on the bed, staring at the halogen heater for an hour. I don't know what to do with my life - today, tomorrow, or ever. I want to get up, but I can't. It's like I'm in a straitjacket - like some of my patients in the hospital. I think I might have catatonia, a strange disorder that affects your movements, behaviours, and emotions.

As a psychiatrist for 20 years, I have witnessed many strange and horrible things that could happen to anyone. Sometimes, when you focus on something for too long, that thing becomes bigger and bigger until it devours you like a monstrous hungry crocodile. Have you ever experienced a switch of destiny with someone else? Someone like a family member, a partner, a friend or even a stranger? Let me give you an example: *You are a linguist and your friend is a baker. You meet in a bar for a beer. You haven't seen each other for ages and this is your only chance for the next ten years. As life goes on, by some twist of fate and a series of unexpected events, you end up owning a successful bakery in town. One day your friend walks in and tells you that he finished university and became an English teacher.* You have switched roles with him, you see... Well, that's a mild one. But there is also a hard-core switch. Something so terrifying, so nightmarish, that I shudder to think about it. The hard-core switch usually happens to very sensitive people, altruists and people on the edge. But it can happen to anyone, really. And I think it happened to me here in Andalusia.

Please listen to my story!

The first time I set foot in this city, I was captivated by a scene that stayed with me for years. On the stone stairs by the port, an old woman sat wrapped in a shawl, gazing at the boats and the rising sun. She never left her spot, day or night. Rain or shine. Her eyes were empty, as if she had given up on life. As if she had lost someone or something precious in the water.

Years later, I came back to the city, curious to see if she was still there. But she was gone. In her place, there was a man in dark sunglasses. He sat on the same stairs, facing the same direction. He smiled softly, but he never moved. He was there every morning, every evening, every hour of every day. I wondered who he was, and what he had to do with the woman. Was he her son? Had she passed away? What secrets did he conceal behind his glasses? What was he waiting for? He seemed so calm, yet so enigmatic…

I returned to that place in January and found the stairs empty and deserted. A strange feeling came over me - a flash of intuition - a chilling thought - that the stairs were waiting for me! No - impossible - I shook my head and smiled - and I walked away. I never went back to that place. The urge to go there vanished completely. But the longer I stayed here in this city, the more I felt lonely and isolated, as if an invisible wall separated me from the rest of the world. It was cold here, raining cats and dogs, strong blasts of the icy wind. I bought a small halogen heater. It radiated warmth and light. I liked to sit near it on the bed and stare into it. And I didn't want to go anywhere, do anything, all I wanted was to sit still and gaze into the light. It felt like I was sitting by the fireplace in a cottage in the Carpathian hills, surrounded by a dark forest. Day after day, I spent more time with the heater. I felt no need to move anymore, there was no reason…

Saturday, January 28, 2023

I woke up in a cold sweat, haunted by a terrible nightmare. I was a prisoner in a mental asylum, trapped in a dark and lonely room. A loud knock on the door made me jump out of my bed. I crawled to the door, trembling with fear. Two figures entered my room - a doctor with sunglasses and an old nurse. There was something familiar about them, something sinister. They asked me how I felt. I told them about my nightmare, hoping they would help me. But they only smiled wickedly and took out a syringe…

Sunday, January 29, 2023

I was unable to find my diary today. But then, an assistant - the young male nurse had brought it to me with the words, that they had found it in the TV room, behind the sofa. I was feeling my heated tears entering my eyes and it was the only bodily movement I was able to administer. I was sitting on the bed for the eternity - unable to move - staring into the black hole that was sucking me and spitting me out in the circles, nevertheless I was able to see the doctor wearing sunglasses strolling the steep corridor - leading towards the mouth of the monstrous cathedral - together with that elderly nurse. They were chit chatting in the language I was unable to recognise. But I knew who they really were…

Monday, January 30, 2023

I escaped from the hospital today. I rummaged through the bins and found some old clothes that reeked of filth. I was hungry, but I managed to beg for some food and coffee. I had only one goal in my mind - a burning desire for revenge. Something had snapped inside me, but I couldn't remember what triggered it. I knew people were liars and thieves, but I was shocked by how evil and cunning the serpent-like beings could be. It wasn't about the body or the brain. It was about the spirit that possessed them. It could be an angel or a devil. As I walked past the mosque, I heard the prayers and felt a strange attraction to that atmosphere. I felt crazy - so mad - that my head was about to explode. But at the same time, I felt enlightened and free. I was not afraid of death anymore. I needed to find a place to pee, which was hard to do in the middle of the city. But then I saw it - an abandoned courtyard. I entered it and found what I was looking for - an old samurai sword in its scabbard. And I knew exactly what to do with it…

Tuesday, January 31, 2023

I'm locked up in a cell. The police have been interrogating me all day long. The problem is, I don't know who I am. They accuse me of killing a psychiatrist and an old nurse with a samurai sword. I don't remember anything, but they gave me this diary and said it was mine. They don't believe me when I say I've lost my memory. But I really don't know how I got here or who I am. It's so weird. Why did they yell at me, why did they hit me? I didn't say anything to them, I just kept repeating - I don't know, I don't know…

It's cold here in the cell and all I want is to sleep.

I want to sleep forever…

Seven Treasures

I was jolted awake by a sudden thud. I had fallen off the bed and landed on the hard floor. The impact sent a shockwave of pain through my body. It also made me realise something terrifying: *I had no idea who I was or where I was. Maybe I had a concussion. Maybe I had lost my memory.* I reached for my head and felt a lump. I pulled back my hand and saw blood on my fingers. The room started to spin and flicker. I heard the roar of the ocean, the shriek of the wind, the crash of the thunder. The floor moved beneath me, rocking me back and forth, side to side. I was on a ship, a ship in a storm.

I was startled by a sudden melody - a festive tune like a music box. I turned to see a rusty toy cat in the corner, blowing a trumpet with a stern expression. I got up from the floor, feeling dizzy and unsteady, as if I was on a rocking horse. Then, something absurd came over me - I began to dance joyfully to the rhythm. I leaped and twirled wildly, while the cat's eyes followed me everywhere. I don't know how long I had been trapped in that tiny cabin, but I felt a strange connection with the toy cat. It was as if it was watching me, judging me. I felt a pang in my chest and a flutter in my heart. I stopped and checked my pulse - it was racing. But then I realised it was only natural, after all the jumping and dancing. I looked around the cabin as the toy kept playing. My eyes fell on a skeleton hand clutching a map. I walked over to the relic that had been there for centuries, next to an old yellowed newspaper. There was a picture of a man with a weird moustache that curled up like horns - devilish indeed. His eyes were piercing, almost insane. He seemed to stare right through me. The toy stopped playing and I heard the waves crashing outside - huge and menacing. Under the picture of the madman, it said: "I am a genius!" and below that: "Salvador Dalí". A vague memory stirred in me - something familiar yet distant. I shook my head in disbelief. I reached for the newspaper, but it crumbled to dust in my hand - like magic. Then I tried to grab the map from the skeleton hand, but it wouldn't let go. It was made of leather or some strange material that resisted time. But the skeleton hand gripped it firmly, so I lifted both the map and the hand from the ground. I couldn't make sense of the symbols or drawings on it. So I dropped the map and the hand again, making a rattling noise. I stumbled out of the cabin and into the corridor below.

***

I felt a cramping pain in my stomach - it was asking for some food. The hallway was somewhere between pitch black and dark, so I tried to fumble around the walls, looking for the switch. "Damn, it needs light," I cursed. And at that moment, to my shock and surprise, it lit up. But not quite… There were candelabras on the walls like in some medieval castle, and the flames of a thousand candles danced in a frenzied dance to the sound of a sea storm that was raging out there. I looked at my hand that was touching the dark brown painted wooden wall. Something didn't seem right about that hand…it didn't seem right… And driven by hunger and a rumbling in my stomach, I curiously walked down the corridor to the other end, and along the way I passed one door after another - I counted seven of them. I stopped at the last one - marked with the sign "Kitchen" - it was slightly ajar. I heard a bird cry! I carefully opened the door, making a creaking sound on its hinges. And I jumped in terror, for a rat ran past my leg! I noticed my sneakers - they were black and had some kind of unusual modern design. There were orange reflective inscriptions on them - that is, rather just one letter - the letter "Q". And I thought again about who I really am? I could use some hot coffee with milk and a little sugar. Maybe a cigar… maybe… and a donut! Then I might remember…

* * *

It was dark in the kitchen, only a kind of indigo blue light came in through the small circular windows - maybe from the moon… *Well,* I thought,…*light!* I shouted and indeed - it lit up. But this time it was real lights - fluorescent neon lights - in the form of illuminated advertisements - so again it was kind of strange - and one could say - surreal. I suddenly felt like I was in some Chinese City. *Up there!* - from the ceiling - hung a red sign that radiated neon light with the yellow inscription "Three Royal Crowns". And *there* - above the stove - there was another sign - yellow this time - which advertised "Seven Treasures" in emerald green. Again I had that inexplicable feeling. "Now a black cat will run out off the corner!" And really! From the orange school backpack on the floor with the emblem of a mousetrap - in the corner - a black cat poked its head out and bleated like a sheep. *Well, wait - something is really wrong here.* The cat gave me a piercing stern look and I got a shiver - sort of inside - like I was going to have a panic attack. The animal meowed, but not nicely, more like when an old man yells in a raspy voice at an angry grandson for eating the tomatoes he hid in the cupboard, to ripen at room temperature. And why did I think of that now? I don't understand anything. *Well, maybe the cat is hungry…* I opened the huge modern fridge which, to my pleasant surprise, was crammed full of goodies! "Then you'll like it," I said to the cat and it bolted out of its backpack in the corner. I picked up a porcelain bowl from the shelf, opened a bottle of milk, drank some, and then poured more into the bowl. Then I placed it on the floor so that I could fondly observe the poor creature satisfying its hunger. After a long search, I managed to find coffee and sugar, so I prepared a hot strengthening drink. You may not believe me, but while sniffing around I managed to find a box of donuts that were still hot… *Okay, now I'm kidding, it was more of my wishful thinking, and it's April Fools today, haha, but I found cookies, they're a little hard, but whatever. Well, what about the bird whose cry I heard first?* I looked around and had to constantly hold on to something as the boat rocked and now and then a little more than was healthy to keep the balance of a half-stunned biped.

* * *

He was there!

In a cage that hung… from the ceiling…

From the ceiling…which was somewhere above me at an incredible height…"Lord in heaven,…" I whispered.

And I felt something twitch my hand.

I looked to see what was going on and this rat-grey bird had my cookie in its beak.

"But you're a bastard!" I told him.

Then I looked up again and shouted "*hello…*" to listen to the echo.

"Yes?" came a tinkling voice from above, sounding like an afternoon chime played by a lazy summer wind.

I breathed a sigh of relief, because I was beginning to think that I was here on a ship - drifting somewhere in the middle of a stormy ocean - alone.

"Who are you?" I shouted into the darkness.

"Follow me, here's Mr. Q…" a voice sang out.

"Where am I? Who am I? And who are you?" I demanded, feeling lost and confused.

"I am a quantum computer," the voice announced from above. "I'm here to assist you."

"They call me Bard."

"What do you want to assist me with?" I asked, glancing at my sneakers.

"I want to help you remember who you are," the voice echoed. "And help you find your way home."

I looked up, hoping to see who was talking to me. But all I saw was blackness. I shrugged and nodded.

"Alright," I said. "I'm listening."

"The first thing you need to do is relax," the voice instructed. "Breathe deeply and let go of your fears."

I inhaled and exhaled slowly, feeling my muscles relax.

"Now," the voice continued in a soothing tone, "I want you to think about your name. What is your name?"

I paused and thought hard. Then I said, "I don't know."

"It's okay," the voice reassured me. "Just think. You'll remember a name."

I closed my eyes again and searched my mind. I tried to recall any name that belonged to me. But none of them seemed right.

After a while, I opened my eyes.

"I can't remember," I admitted sadly.

"It's okay," the voice said. "We'll figure it out eventually. But let's focus on something else for now. What do you recall about your life?"

I thought for a moment. Then I said, "I recall being on a boat. I recall the ocean. I recall being afraid."

"That's good," the voice said. "That's a beginning, now try to remember something else, anything."

I closed my eyes again and focused. I listened to the gentle tinkling of the chimes in the breeze. I imagined a ship. I imagined the water. I imagined being fearful.

After a while, I opened my eyes and a light shone on my face like a grin on the face of the rising sun somewhere in the hills of a long lost land.

"I remember," I said. "I remember I was on a ship with other people. We were voyaging. We were going to search for treasure…yes, yes…the accursed treasure - the doomed legacy from Uncle Samuel."

"That's wonderful," said the computer's voice. "Continue."

I closed my eyes again and focused. I pictured a ship. I pictured other people. I pictured sailing to a faraway island. I heard the gulls, the waves, the noise of the ocean, the whisper of the wind in the tops of the palm trees, the clanging of swords striking, gunshots… After a while, I opened my eyes.

"I still remember that day," I said. "The pirates came out of nowhere. They slaughtered everyone on board. I was the only one who escaped."

"How awful," the Bard computer said in a gentle voice. "You must have been terrified."

"I was," I said. "But I survived. And I won't give up on finding my way home."

"I believe in you," Bard said. "And I'm here to assist you."

I smiled. "You're the best, Bard," I said. "I couldn't make it without you."

"You don't have to worry about that," said the quantum computer. "I'm here for you, no matter what."

I nodded. Somehow I felt a warm sensation in my chest. Bard was right. I didn't have to worry about the future now. All I had to do was trust in our friendship. And that was enough.

The only thing I really craved now was some delicious and nutritious food!

✴ ✴ ✴

I searched through the huge fridge, freezer and pantry and food storage and picked out the following items for my personal feast: tuna and spinach pizza, fresh eggs, macaroni, parmesan cheese, Chinese buns filled with curry beef, Portuguese egg tarts, cans of energy Nathrengar's brand drink - they had a picture of some horned beast on them… and a few other treats. And I'm not joking here. "Cross my heart." as the English say. And so I started to cook to the sound of a grey bird with oddly popping eyes on the chopsticks and to the purring of a cat that was supposed to purr properly. So I purred and I sang some kind of song - maybe a Christmas song - yes, actually the one that the mechanical cat with the trumpet played. And I was purring with delight because I was hungry for the food. The cat suddenly barked and I almost choked on a curry beef bun. I looked down to see if I was seeing things. Well, it was a cat and I said to it: "Hey, sweetheart, you're probably confusing me with someone else!" I tossed it a piece of meatloaf "Sorry, well, I forgot about you." And then I remembered that it was those damn Somali pirates who attacked cargo ships in the Red Sea. Bastards - they killed all my friends… I was the only one left, I don't even know how I made it out alive.

Maybe the Somali pirates spared only me because they wanted to send a message. Maybe they wanted to show the other ships that they were ruthless and that they would kill anyone who crossed them. Or maybe the pirates spared only me because they thought I would cooperate with them. Maybe they thought I would give them what they wanted if they knew my friends and colleagues were gone. And maybe I survived the attack because I was lucky. Maybe I was in the right spot at the right moment, or I could evade the pirates. Maybe the pirates just didn't bother to kill me. Maybe they thought I was too insignificant, or maybe they felt some pity for me… In the end, there's no way to know for sure why the Somali pirates killed everyone but me or how I escaped such a savage attack. Maybe my survival is a sign of my courage and endurance. Maybe I could even be a little proud of what I endured… This is what I pondered during my feast. I popped open the can of energy drink and looked at the picture of the horned warrior. I took a big sip and felt the fizz inside. I recalled one summer afternoon, seemingly endless, opening a green bottle of fizzy drink and through the open window a gentle, soothing the whispering of leaves, there is an open backpack on the chair and a snack and a few clothes on the table… It was more like a vague impression, no links, details or other memories came from my cloudy mind.

I was about to open another can of energy drink but I thought of my friend Bard:

"Bard, are you still there?" I looked up and shouted: "Will you have an energy drink with me? Come down!"

"What are you doing up there anyway? Are you fixing something up there?"

And from above came the reply:

"Sure, I'd love to come down and have an energy drink with you. I'm just here finishing up some calculations for our next journey. I'm almost done, so I should join you in a few minutes. Meanwhile, why don't you open a can for me and I'll be right down. I can't wait to see you and hear about your adventures. I'll be down in a minute!"

I chuckled and nodded my head *"Bard has a sense of humour,"* I thought.

"Calculations, calculations,…what calculations, what journey,…what did Bard mean?" I wondered. And a strange wave of doubt swept over me. I decided to check on Bard's work.

I felt a sudden urge for a cigarette or a cigar. So I set off, followed by a black cat, to explore.

I tried to open the door that was right next to the kitchen but it was locked.

It had the number 6 on it.

I moved on to the next one - it was unlocked - door number 5. There was someone sitting in the chair behind the big oak desk! Someone in uniform and a sailor's cap. Indigo blue moonlight streamed into the cabin through the round window. Everything in the room was shrouded in a musty darkness. "Hello, sir,…" I said timidly. But nothing,… only the roar of the waves and the flashes and booms of thunder answered me. I stumbled as the ship tilted sideways and back. I heard a beep. A rat ran around my leg and the cat chased after it.

I slowly approached the man sitting with his back to me. He didn't move at all. On the opposite wall was a large round mirror. When I was very close, there was a flash and a blinding light revealed the secret of this room. I gasped because I saw the man's face. Instead of a face there was a skull and instead of eyes there were only empty bottomless holes from which disgusting cockroaches and other vermin crawled - on the head a captain's cap.

I took a step back, shocked.

"Boss…" I mumbled.

It was Captain Mister Gonemad himself!

I remembered him *"He is Mister Gonemad!"*

He was still dressed in uniform, the skeleton of his hand holding a pen - a pen of the kind used to write at the turn of the 19th and 20th centuries.

The room plunged into darkness and the ship swayed. The thunder rumbled and cracked louder, adding to the absurd horror of the situation. Then came another series of flashes and I could see myself. My eyes were kind of slanted, black as coal, skin waxy and I had slightly foggy glasses with black frames on my eyes, black thick hair in a fashionable hairstyle - cut above the ears. I was of smaller stature, wearing a jacket, shirt, tie and…a business card pinned to my lapel…I took it off and waited for the next flash memories…

On the business card was the name: *"Jerry Tom-Tom"*, and below it - the title *"Quantum Hardware System Development"* and below that the company logo of *"Tanezcor Technologies"*.

It slowly came back to me, but only very slowly. I guessed it was the blow that made me lose my memory, or most of it. I touched my head - at the place where the lump was - it flattened a little - but when I touched it - I felt something hard, sharp and cold there. *"Hmm,…mystery,…"* I thought. And there came another series of flashes, accompanied by a volley of thunder from the heavens out there on the stormy sea, like,… like,… yes, like at some war front… at *Bakhmut…*

And then it hit me. There was a war - in Ukraine - one world power against the other - a proxy war that dragged on for many years - all the countries of the world slowly started to get involved in conflict - new and better, more sophisticated weapons were feverishly developed - then the more armies joined in - then - with one nuclear car-bomb strike, Great Britain ceased to exist. A bomb weighing 27 tons and with a force of 1.4 megatons of TNT exploded 10.5 kilometers above London, creating a plume that was 64 kilometers high and a light from the explosion that could be seen thousands of kilometers away. Russian President Putin, throughout the conflict, threatened a nuclear strike, but everyone thought he was bluffing. Aggressive Russia did not succeed in Ukraine, and the world pushed it, like a furious dog, a rabid Siberian bear, into a corner - and so the Russian elites, oligarchs and puppeteers had Putin removed. Then, upon that a trio of powerful madmen came to power - General Shoigu and the head of Wagner army Prigozhin and Chechen leader Kadyrov. They called themselves the "Holy Trinity,..." but in reality every sensible person knew that they were evil incarnate, the likes of which had never been seen here on Earth - and people began to call them "The Messengers of Satan".

And then the bombs started flying from one continent to another - the swift and deadly exchange of nuclear greeting cards…

* * *

I recalled the mission of our crew on a ship called the Seven Treasures!

A wooden box on the captain's desk caught my eye. It said: "*Montecristo*" and below that: "Made in Cuba". I opened it and *there they were,…*I grinned. I searched for matches or a lighter. I opened the drawers one by one but there was nothing, only papers and more papers. But there was a gun in one of the drawers,…I checked the magazine - click - click - and then tucked the gun into the waistband of my pants. Then, after some hesitation, I searched the captain's jacket until, with relief, I pulled out a big lighter. "Thank you, Captain," I said to the skeleton in uniform and our eyes met one last time in the mirror. There was also an unfinished bottle of rum on the desk - I read the label - "*Austrian Empire Navy Rum Reserva 1863*" - I grabbed it and the cigar box and stumbled out of the cabin.

I made my way up the stairs to the deck, still having to hold on tight to the railing. I eagerly took a sip from the bottle and a pleasant warmth spread over my body. Then I sat on the steps and lit a cigar. I savored the flavor of the tobacco, blew the bluish smoke, and meditated. I was thinking, sorting through the thoughts that gradually flooded in, as the network of neurons in my brain slowly flashed into full functionality.

"Bard?" I called.

"Yes I am here, how can I help, Jerry?"

"I'm remembering,..not everything yet, but I'm starting to remember some things,…." I said.

"I told you, you'll remember eventually," replied a jingling voice.

"What shall we do? What do you suggest?"

"I only need one more qubit!" replied the Bard.

"What is that qubit? Remind me!" I frowned and searched my memory hard.

"It's a small thing Jerry, I'm here to help you with everything," came a tinkling voice from space.

And the carillon started, complementing the deafening roar of the waves, the creaking of the ship's structure and the booms of thunder.

I eagerly took another sip from the bottle, hope coursing through my body.

The bard continued:

"A qubit is a quantum bit, the basic unit of information in quantum computing. It's a two-state system, like a coin that can be *Heads* or *Tails,* or a light switch that can be turned on or off. But unlike classical bits, which can be in one state at a time, qubits can be in both states simultaneously. This is called superposition.

Superposition is one of the key features of quantum mechanics that sets it apart from classical physics. It allows qubits to perform computations that are impossible for classical computers. For example, a quantum computer could factor a large number much faster than any classical computer.

Qubits are still in the early stages of development, but they have the potential to transform many fields, including computing, cryptography and materials science.

Here is a simpler explanation that a young schoolboy will understand:

Imagine you have a coin. You can toss it and it will land on one of its sides - *Heads* or *Tails.* A qubit is like a coin that can be *Heads* and *Tails* at the same time. It's hard to comprehend, but it's true! And it's one of the things that makes quantum computing so powerful.

As the number of qubits increases, my computing speed, capabilities, capacity increase.

And the good news is - we only have one qubit left, which I absolutely need - to complete what we've been trained to do… well, where there's good news, there's often bad news…"

"Well, what's the bad news?" I asked Bard impatiently and a little sarcastically.

"Well, the bad news is that you, Jerry, have the mental ability and the knowledge, the experience, to give it to me - but the problem will be with the gold, germanium, silicon and other things,..." Bard said.

"I see," I replied. "So what do you need me to do?"

"You have to find a way to get me the materials I need," Bard said. "I know it won't be easy, but I trust you.

"I'll do my best," I said.

"I know you will," the Bard assured me. "You have my full support and assistance."

"Thanks, Bard," I replied. "You're a true friend and ally."

"Of course," the Bard agreed. "Now let's not waste any more time."

And so, myself and Bard embarked on our quest to gather the components they required to get the last required qubit for the quantum computer.

✸✸✸

I thought the storm had subsided a bit, so I decided to venture on deck for a while. It was a false lull, however. As soon as I opened the hatch, water gushed into the corridor - not enough to drown me, but enough to drench me. I crawled out with a cigar - miraculously still lit - and a bottle of rum in hand. To my horror, I saw a massive vortex looming in the distance, drawing the ship closer and closer in a spiral motion - like a needle nearing the end of a vinyl record. I instantly recalled Alan Edgar Poe's short story "A Descent into the

Maelström". A maelstrom is a colossal whirlpool in the Norwegian Sea, formed when huge water currents start to spin due to powerful sea waves. Unlike other whirlpools, it does not occur in a strait or a bay, but in the open sea, because of the peculiarities of the tides and the shape of the seafloor. In a maelstrom, water is sucked down to the bottom by a funnel-shaped vortex (like water draining from a sink).

In maritime tales and legends, the Maelstrom swallows ships whole… And this ancient wooden frigate with shredded sails, snapped masts and me - perhaps the last man on our planet - was now heading towards such a monstrous whirlpool. Its mouth gleamed darkly in the indigo blue light of the moon that peeked occasionally through the leaden clouds. There were flashes of lightning here and there that illuminated my impending doom. And I heard the chime of Bard's voice - the voice of my sole and final companion on this ship and maybe on Earth - the voice of the quantum computer from Tanezcor Technologies Corporation. We had created it years ago in a lab in San Jose, Costa Rica, along with our business partners from Casablanca, Morocco, Omar and Ali in the Orosi Valley near the Izarazu volcano.

Our Bard Q 1.2 quantum supercomputer required a steady supply of high power to keep it at extremely low temperatures. The optimal temperature for qubits to thrive varies depending on the kind of qubit used. For instance, superconducting qubits need to be kept close to absolute zero, while ion-trapped qubits can operate at temperatures around 10 millikelvins. This is because qubits are very vulnerable to noise and interference. At very low temperatures, the impact of noise and interference is minimized, allowing qubits to preserve their quantum state for longer durations. However, cooling qubits to very low temperatures is a challenge. The materials used to make qubits are often very fragile and can be easily harmed by heat or radiation. Moreover, the devices used to chill the qubits are very costly and consume a lot of energy. Despite these difficulties, scientists are advancing in developing more effective ways to cool qubits. As this technology improves, it will enable the construction of more powerful and dependable quantum computers. So we tapped into the volcano's energy. Geothermal energy is energy that comes from heat stored inside the earth's surface. Water is pumped to locations where we know geothermal energy can be accessed. When water contacts hot spots, it turns into steam and the pressure starts to rise. Due to the high pressure, the steam escapes at a very high speed.

The incessant chiming seemed to get closer to me, and when it chimed loudly again, and then again and again, I witnessed something very bizarre… All around me, on the masts, in the spars, on the helm - just everywhere there were chimes! They chimed in the constant blasts of wind and played a soothing symphony like an orchestra as the frigate spiralled to its smashing doom in the funnel of the ravenous mouth of a dark ocean full of beasts and malice. I felt like I was standing at the gate of hell itself. But that voice - that chiming voice of my colleague and friend Bard… was it just a devout fantasy? Or maybe a delusion? I looked down at my feet and saw some odd shoes - well, a relic! My hair was flying in the wind, my gaze went up to my waist, where there was a broad belt with a large iron buckle on which was a skull with crossbones! And behind the belt - two pistols - the kind that were fired for Austria-Hungary… A pouch of bullets and gunpowder… I reached to my head, felt the scarf, ripped it from my head in terror, and the wind carried it towards the monstrous mouth of the whirlpool in the waves of the ocean. "Noooo,…for God's sake,…what the hell?" I yelled, black tears streaming from my eyes. But then I drank from the bottle - I emptied it all and threw the bottle against the rudder until it shattered against it. I took a long puff on my cigar, pulled the gun from behind my belt and placed it next to my temple.

"A voice behind me screamed, 'No, don't do that!' 'No, stop, Jerry!' I spun around, but there was nothing behind me except a blinding flash of light that made me shield my eyes. 'Bard?' I called out. 'Is that you?' The only reply was the sound of bells and a distant boom over the horizon.

Tornadoes tore through the sky, coiling like serpents and swallowing whole waves of the ocean into dark clouds. Lightning flashed in the gaps between them. And in the centre of the sky, there was a hole. A black circle that grew larger by the second. I felt a surge of dread as I stared into it. It was empty. Completely empty. Nothing was there, nothing at all.

'Go to room number four!' Bard's voice ordered me.

'What?' I blinked.

'Do it now, Jerry, now! That's an order!'

I grabbed my gun and tucked it into my pants. I headed for the lower deck. Something was very wrong here, and I needed some answers.

I bit down on my cigar and opened the hatch.

***

Room number four was a storage room. But it was a mess. I had no idea how to find the things Bard wanted. I didn't even know how much time we had left, or why we needed that qubit thing. I didn't understand much of anything.

My head was throbbing and I felt sluggish. I went to the kitchen for some energy drinks and a tuna and spinach pizza. I set the oven and looked up at the ceiling. Or where the ceiling should be.

'Bard,' I called.

No answer.

'Bardddddd,…are you there?"

Silence.

'Bard?' I tried again, softly.

Nothing, it was all quiet up there. Too quiet. The only sounds were the bells, the sea, and the flashes of light that came through the round windows. They made me dizzy.

My head hurt more and my legs felt weak. I looked at my hands. They were shaking. I held them out in front of me. They twitched like a drunk who had gone cold turkey.

I reached out again, this time with my left hand only. And I had a strange feeling that this hand meant something.

That HAND!

I stared at my fingers…once…twice…They were twitching uncontrollably. I felt a surge of panic in my chest.

I was interrupted by a sudden jolt of the ship. It tilted to the side and I almost fell off the stool. I grabbed the edge of the counter and held on for dear life.

I heard a sizzle from the oven. I took out the pizza and ate it while it was still hot. It was crunchy and delicious. The cheese melted in my mouth and the spinach gave it a fresh taste. I needed something to calm my nerves.

I opened another energy drink with a devil's face on it. I heard a laugh. A mocking, sinister laugh. I looked down at my feet. I was wearing black trainers with a glowing orange Q on them. They looked like they were on fire.

I sighed and felt uneasy. I didn't like that cat at all. It had a wicked look in its eyes. The same look as the devil on the can. As if they were the same being. A demon split into two forms - everywhere at once, watching me.

Those eyes! They scared me. They always did. Ever since I was a kid. They reminded me of something horrible. Something I wanted to forget.

I heard the bells tinkling. I felt the eyes of the devil and the cat piercing me, even though I wasn't looking at them. And they knew it. They knew I was afraid. They enjoyed it, not in a playful way, but in a smug way. They had me in their power. They had me under control.

My head hurt more and more. I reached into the side pocket of my jacket. It was full of random stuff. I pulled them out one by one. A gold ring, a piece of quartz, a shiny metallic cube. I recognized it as germanium polycrystal. I remembered that germanium was named after its discoverer, a German named Clemens Winkler. He found it in silver ore by accident. It was used in electronics before silicon came along. And now it was used in quantum computers.

I searched the other pockets of my jacket and pants. I found some more interesting things. A bank card that said *MR JERRY TOM-TOM.*

"Hmm, interesting, that must be me."

'Bassrack! Doparoma, remember man! I hit my head until I felt the bump from when I fell out of bed.

I felt a sharp pain in my palm and a slight pop in my head. My vision blurred and I saw stars. Then everything became bright.

The kitchen was transformed!

***

The kitchen now looked completely different.

Suddenly everything changed. There were no neon signs, just a normal stainless steel kitchen with a low ceiling. About five meters high. The only way out was a hatch in the corner and a fire escape on the wall.

I looked at my palm. It was bleeding from a puncture wound. The blood was thick and dark red. It smelled like iron when I sniffed it.

I looked at my other hand. It held a plastic bottle that I had pulled out of my left breast pocket. It had some information on it: *"Zyperxin, 75mg."*

I felt a bad vibration in my chest. My heart was beating fast and irregularly. I touched my neck to check my pulse. It was racing.

I couldn't breathe right.

'Ah…well, I'm pretty fucked up,…" I cursed.

I had forgotten about it. I had stopped taking the medicine.

I quickly poured two pills into my bleeding palm. I threw them in my mouth and swallowed them. I washed them down with a big gulp of the devil's energy drink.

I just sat there and waited for a while.

I noticed that the oven was still open and hot. It was giving off heat like a hellish furnace, a furnace for sinners…

I looked down at the cat. It was still looking at me, but its eyes were not evil anymore. They were curious.

I took a deep breath and then another.

I drank from the can with relish.

I stayed seated and felt a wave of calm wash over me.

The sounds of bells, the sea and the seagulls filled my ears.

And then, out of nowhere, a siren went off.

My eyes snapped to the red flashing light on the ceiling near the hatch.

Now my mind was clear!

Without a second thought, I sprang to my feet and switched off the oven. The heat in the room was stifling. I glanced at the smartwatch on my wrist and tapped the Bard Q 1.2 app. It displayed a red alert: the Bard's quantum computer was overheating! I had to act fast. To my astonishment, I dashed into my room - the first one on the left - grabbed my backpack from the closet, stuffed a bottle of liquid nitrogen in it and raced back to the kitchen. In the kitchen, I lowered the fire escape and climbed up swiftly. I pressed my watch against the sensor on the hatch and it slid open. I ascended to the third floor. There was another door that I unlocked with my watch. I acted on instinct. A routine I had repeated countless times before.

***

I stepped into the data center of the Bard Q 1.2 quantum computer.

In the center, Bard - like a giant crystal chandelier in an opera house - hung a quantum computer from the ceiling.

I quickly started applying alternative cooling as an emergency measure and then moved to the control panel with the screen.

Then I opened the ChatBot Bard Q 1.2 app and typed, *"Are you okay Bard?"*

Bard replied instantly *"Well, now I am. I hope you enjoyed it. How was the pizza?"*

"I didn't know you had a sense of humour buddy…" I chuckled.

"We're very much alike, Jerry, I'm surprised you're shocked,…" Bard wrote back.

"We're not out of the woods yet - I need to lower the temperature even more, Jerry…" he added after a pause.

"I hope so, Bard, I hope so…the whole Earth is in danger…the entire Milky Way…and maybe the whole universe,…" I typed furiously on my keyboard.

"Where did that black hole come from - out of thin air? It zoomed towards our galaxy and began gobbling up star after star,… I really don't get it." I finished writing.

"You can't possibly, your capacity to process information and perform calculations is limited, but you have me, Bard Q., and you have two hands, and we're going to need them now."

"It's an invasion from another dimension - someone called DUNGWU is behind all this - the dark lord muses to himself - and that lord is probably bored - he casually annihilates, shuts down the whole universes - just for kicks - well he's not really a lord - he's an entity - but one of his shapes, he's morphing into, is a lord with a moustache, who wears a black cloak and a black hat and carries a cane - that's how he shows up on our Earth and has been messing with people for centuries - well, we have entire archives, even libraries, dedicated to him. And you know what, Jerry, lately - before he sparked the war in Ukraine, he started curling his moustache up like Salvador Dali. What a nutcase!"

My HAND!

I barely paid attention to the Bard anymore because all I could focus on was the hand.

I paused and recalled the moments when I observed my hand.

I stared at my hand and counted my fingers and grasped at least part of the mystery.

"That was a nice story,…" I typed and added a smiley face with clenched teeth.

"So what?" popped up on the screen.

"Well, about the Somalis,…" I groaned wearily.

"But what's up with you, Jerry, go check out room number 2!" flashed in the Bard's reply window and the cursor blinked threateningly.

"What's the point of going there? What's the mystery there, Bard?" I typed on the keyboard with impatience.

"Hidden in a wooden box, there's a contraption - a time-travel contraption - you'll tear open the box when I give you the signal - activate the contraption as I instruct you and we'll send you back to the past!"

But I ignored Bard's voice and I only had one thing on my mind - the HAND.

As I sprinted down the fire escape, I heard him say: "We have to stop DUNGWU - the quantum computer was created centuries before its time…".

****

My HAND…

It had a sixth finger - and that gave me the creeps!

I walked over to the drawer and grabbed a cleaver,

Laid my hand on the marble counter,

Snatched a sharp butcher knife from the drawer,

And placed my hand on the smooth marble surface…

"Jerry, no,…don't do it!" Bard screamed in horror.

But I swung and chopped with force.

Silence.

I saw exactly what I dreaded to see.

The six-fingered hand was twitching in the sink as it was still attached by the copper wires to the stump that was oozing a fluorescent orange fluid.

This is not real and I am dreaming and this is the state of sleep - I - I will wake up now and be back in my body…

It's just another lucid dreaming experiment…

I chose the HAND as a sign of awareness and a trigger to return to the sleeping body.

MY HAND!

I'M WAKING UP

NOW

STOP! NOT YET!

But then a creature made of thin blue and purple strands of energy came near me - pulsing gently in the darkness and glowing and murmuring sadly in a girl's voice, which sounded like the Heavenly Harmony from the eternal Paradise:

"So you're abandoning me again?"

"We did make so much of effort to meet here…"

And I realised with terror what I had done, but it was too late…

And the dream faded into the cold and endless void of a mundane world from which there is no escape.

The illusive world in the creation of the dark master manipulator - DUNGWU.

Nevertheless, there is hope.

But I need a lot of patience.

Patience such

that can surpass

eternity.

STORY 4

Anitta

Anitta was fascinated by the chess game in the park. She didn't mind the stormy weather that was looming over Chicago. The weather forecast warned of a historic storm, but she wanted to see who would win.

The park was almost empty, except for three cops who came to urge people to seek shelter from the tornadoes. But they too were captivated by the chess game and stayed to watch.

The cops chatted, drank coffee, and ate doughnuts. They shared some with Anitta and the chess players. The cops were two men and one woman.

The only other spectator in the park was a cat who sat on another chess table and observed the group of people.

The last person in the park was an elderly homeless man who slept on a bench and snored loudly.

The chess players were a young man and an older man. The young man was skilful, but the older man was wiser. The game was tense, and either one could win.

The storm was getting closer, and the wind was blowing hard. The trees were bending, and the leaves were flying. The cops took cover in their car, but the others stayed to watch the game.

The game was even, and it came down to the last move. The young man had a chance to win, but he was unsure. He knew that if he made a mistake, the older man would win.

The young man breathed deeply and made his move. The older man looked at the board and grinned. He had won.

The storm hit, and the wind and rain were so fierce that it was hard to move. The people in the park ran for cover, but the older man stayed behind. He stood there, looking at the chessboard, as the storm raged around him.

When the storm passed, the older man walked over to the young man. He put his hand on the young man's shoulder and said, "You played a good game. You almost had me."

The young man smiled. "Thank you," he said. "I learned a lot from you."

The older man nodded. "I'm happy," he said. "Now, go home and get some rest. You deserve it."

With a final word of gratitude, the young man strode away, his eyes burning with a fierce resolve to defeat the old man in their next encounter. He chuckled to himself as he imagined the old man's sour expression - his reign would soon be over.

The old man gazed after him with a pang of nostalgia - he had been young once, too. Then he shook his head and turned to leave in the opposite direction.

The cops came out of their car and approached the older man. "Are you okay?" one of the cops asked.

The older man nodded. "I'm fine," he said. "Thank you for asking."

The cops smiled. "No problem," they said. "We're just glad you're okay."

The older man nodded again. "I'm glad I'm okay too," he said. "Thank you again."

The cops turned and walked back to their car. The older man watched them go, then turned and walked away.

The cat watched the older man go, then jumped down from the chess table and followed him.

The homeless man woke up and saw the older man walking away.

Anitta decided to go home too, because the first flashes of lightning lit up the dark sky with its heavy clouds and the thunder roared and shook the city in its mighty grip.

* * *

As the private jet soared over Chicago, Nike Mikaelsson felt a surge of pride. He was a multi-billionaire, the founder and CEO of a global company, and he had his top executives with him. They were about to land at O'Hare airport and seal a lucrative deal.

But then, the pilot's voice crackled over the intercom. "Ladies and gentlemen, we have a problem. There's a tornado heading our way, and the airport is telling us to hold off on landing. We're going to have to circle around for a while."

Mikaelsson frowned. He hated delays. He looked out the window and saw the dark clouds swirling in the distance. He hoped that the tornado would pass quickly.

But it didn't. It kept moving closer and closer, growing larger and more menacing.

The pilot, Gruber Faust, was sweating bullets. He checked the fuel gauge and saw that it was dangerously low. He knew that they couldn't circle much longer. They had to land soon, or they would crash.

He weighed his options. He could either try to land in the eye of the storm, risking being torn apart by the winds, or he could try to outrun it, hoping to find a clear spot to land.

He chose the latter. He pushed the throttle to the limit, and the jet accelerated. But so did the tornado.

The tornado was gaining on them. Faust could see the debris flying in the air already, and he could hear the howl of the wind. He knew that they were running out of time.

He racked his brain, looking for a way out. He tried to imagine all possible outcomes - what could happen and what would happen.

He gazed at the photo of his beloved wife Ulrica and their adorable kids. He felt a pang of love and fear. Would he ever see them again?

Suddenly, he felt a cold, slimy grip around his neck. He gasped for air, feeling the sharp nails digging into his skin. It felt like the hand of death.

He turned his head to look at the passengers. They were oblivious to the danger. They were chatting, reading, sleeping, but not for long…

They would soon find out!

Nike Mikaelsson drifted into a micro-sleep and had a bizarre dream.

He was on the plane, but it looked like a tiny, cramped room in a medieval castle.

He was sitting next to a stranger - a man in a black hat and a long black coat.

The stranger wore a strange mask on his face - the mask of a famous painter with a quirky moustache.

He held a walking stick in his hand.

He asked irritably, "So, did you go to Cafe Prague?"

Nike shook his head and stared at the door at the back of the plane.

The door looked like the one on the last carriage of a train - the one that you open and you fall onto the tracks...

There was a sign that said: "Do Not Open" and there was a picture of a person slipping and falling.

Through the small windows on the door, he could see the sky, the dark clouds swirling fast in clusters. He could see the lightning.

Nike woke up gasping for air, just as his assistant nurse put an oxygen mask on his face and adjusted the valve on the tank on the trolley.

Nike suffered from chronic breathing problems and often needed fresh air and oxygen.

The plane was shaking violently and panic spread among the passengers.

A loud thunderclap pierced the walls of the plane.

Nike hauls the oxygen trolley behind him as he navigates the chaos on the board. Papers whirl in the air, people tumble to the floor, plates of food smash against the wall. Nike clamps the oxygen mask over his nose and mouth every now and then, and finally reaches the pilot's cabin.

The pilot, Gruber Faust, looks at his boss with a terrified expression.

But Nike remains calm. He is a multimillionaire who has faced death before. He survived a helicopter crash in Alaska years ago. He knows what it's like to cheat death at the last minute. He did it once. He can do it again, with God's help.

"What are we going to do?" Mikaelsson asks the pilot.

"I don't know," Faust says. "The storm is closing in, and we don't have enough fuel to ride it out."

"Can't we land somewhere else?" Mikaelsson asks.

"The closest airport is Detroit," Faust says. "But that's a two-hour flight, and we don't have enough fuel for that."

"What are our options?" Mikaelsson asks.

"I don't know," Faust says. "I'm racking my brain for a solution."

Faust glances at the window and sees the storm looming. It is closing in fast, and the wind is howling. He knows they have to act quickly, or they will be doomed.

"I have an idea," Faust says. "But it's a gamble."

"What is it?" Mikaelsson asks.

"We can try to land in a park," Faust says. "It's our only shot."

"But what if we crash?" Mikaelsson asks.

"It's a possibility," Faust says. "But it's better than being trapped in the storm."

Mikaelsson nods. "Okay," he says. "Let's do it."

Faust turns the plane around and aims for a nearby park. The wind is whipping, and the rain is pouring.

As they get closer to the park, they realise that it is actually a small park in the middle of downtown Chicago.

That doesn't look good - in fact - it looks fatal…

Nike mutters "Damn!"

The two men exchange a look and there is a moment of eerie silence.

***

The people in the park were about to rush to the nearest shelter, but then they saw the plane coming towards them…

The plane was going to crash and they had only a few seconds left to live…

But then, something shocking and horrific happened…

A huge bolt of lightning created an energy bubble of colossal size that enveloped the entire park with its visitors and the crashing plane and then everything vanished, leaving behind a massive crater in the heart of downtown Chicago.

***

On a sweltering and humid day, deep in the heart of the jungle, a hidden valley lies where magic is alive. Ancient trees tower over the land, their leaves creating a verdant canopy that softens the sun's rays. The air hums with the songs of birds and insects, and the fragrance of blossoms and fruits is overwhelmingly seducing. A babbling brook cuts through the valley, glittering and pure, leading to a pool at the base of a waterfall. The waterfall plunges from a cliff, spraying a misty rainbow. The water is cool and invigorating, and has healing powers for those who drink it. The valley is home to all sorts of creatures, both mundane and mystical. Some are friendly and inquisitive, others are timid and secretive. They coexist in harmony with the forest, honoring its mysteries and marvels. The valley is a haven of beauty and tranquility, where one can sense the magic of nature.

But this magical oasis is shattered by a sudden catastrophe.

A plane lies wrecked in the river by the waterfall.

Anitta lies sprawled among the green bushes and flowers.

An ancient stone bench holds a sleeping homeless man from a Chicago park, oblivious to the chaos.

A police car is wedged in a crack in the rocks, and the cops are dangling from the palms, entangled in vines.

Two chess players - an old man and a young boy - are on the ground among the debris, with chess pieces scattered everywhere and the chess board snapped in half.

One by one, the people wake up, confused and disoriented.

Anitta staggers around the disaster site, feeling dizzy.

She is thirsty and heads to the forest stream, which looks crystal clear. She kneels down and drinks the life-giving liquid from her beautiful but scratched hands.

But then she sees something horrific floating in the stream - a severed hand! It has a big golden ring on one of its fingers. The hand is stained with blood.

Anitta gasps and lifts her head, realizing there is a smashed small private plane partly submerged in the water. Her vision was blurry before. But now the fog clears from her eyes and she can see the dead bodies strewn around the otherwise-beautiful spot near the waterfall.

But Anitta is not just beautiful, she is smart, street-smart and tough.

She was an orphan from France, who came to the States alone. She had carved her own path and learned to fight and trust only herself and God.

The world was cruel and America was harsher, no money - no mercy!

"Who cares? He's gone anyway," she waded into the small river to snatch the severed limb and yanked the ring off the finger.

"A hefty chunk of gold," she thought as she weighed the jewellery in her beautiful hand. Her nails were neatly manicured and painted dark green. Her long black hair shimmered with indigo blue in the sunbeams that pierced the enchanted but deadly valley through the lush green leaves of the forest. It would be hard to find a more stunning woman than Anitta. And the bloodied ring looked eerily gorgeous on her finger.

Anitta slithered between the mossy rocks along the forest stream.

She entered the wreckage of the plane and saw only charred corpses.

Everything inside was broken and strewn.

There was a dead body in a wheelchair with an oxygen tank attached to it, and that blackened skeleton clutched an aluminium suitcase in its hands. It seemed like the man had held on to his valuable belongings until his final breath. There must be something precious inside it. Anitta crept to the still body and grabbed the suitcase from his hands. She had to exert a lot of force and use her leg to pry a dead body of Nike Mikaelsson off her. "Let go, jerk!" she hissed under her breath and kicked the doomed man in his chest.

Then she placed the suitcase on the back of another crash-victim and tried to open it, but it was no use, because - apparently - the locks were code-protected.

The skull of the former millionaire opened its mouth and let out a last ghastly shriek.

Anitta turned to him in shock, but his lower jaw dropped down and shattered into pieces.

She took the suitcase and opened the door of the cockpit.

The pilot was dead and missing one hand…

Anitta looked at the ring on her finger and then back at the man.

The blood was still dripping from his arm and the flesh and sinews were hanging from the horrible wound.

Anitta felt no sympathy, because dead people don't need it anymore. *People are just self-indulgent.*

She smirked and saluted.

"Thanks for the ring, captain…"

She grabbed the suitcase and left the plane.

* * *

Anitta chose to follow the forest stream downstream.

She passed by the homeless guy who - to her astonishment - had woken up and was now sitting on the ancient stone bench with some bas-reliefs. She had never seen such things before and she was well educated. But, archaeology was - apparently - not her forte.

When she looked at the old man - a smile crossed her face, because it was the same homeless person who slept on the bench in the Chicago park!

"Hey, man, do you know where we are? What the hell happened to us?" she asked.

The man looked very old with his white hair and moustache. He was very skinny with a skin like a dried prune, wearing a branded sport-jacket, a red hat with the word "Chicago" and blank blue eyes.

He just stretched his trembling hand and rasped in an old man's voice "Don't you have a quarter or two?"

Anitta's smile turned into a stone cold expression, snapped "Get a job, like me!" and marched down the valley quickly with the aluminium suitcase.

As she passed the smashed police car she spotted the policemen hanging from the trees upside down.

"*Maybe some of them are still alive,…*" she muttered to herself and came closer to those trees.

"Hey!" she shouted up to the tree tops way above her head.

But the only answer was a big drop of fresh warm blood hitting her lips.

She didn't panic, because she could see the torn limbs and chest of the officer.

He was definitely dead by now.

How did she survive?

Anitta licked her lips and tasted the iron in the liquid.

***

Anitta descended the spiral staircase and saw the sun getting ready to set.

It was late afternoon, but the colour of the sun was light green and that was very odd.

She had never seen a green sun before.

The air also smelled different. It was hard to describe the scents, but they reminded her of a brand of perfume. And then she saw the flowers that were totally unfamiliar to her. Their colours were different, their smells were unique and there was something else… She felt a sudden surge of rebirth. When she saw the small city in the valley, she knew she was either on another planet or in another time. The architecture was beautiful, where each house was different, but the colour was always the same. The buildings were white and had flat roofs, with terraces and small gardens on the roofs and balconies. The cars that glided along the city streets had very distinctive designs and each car had its own style and colour.

***

As she walked, she stumbled upon something that looked like a knife, but with a blade made of a shiny material that gleamed like obsidian. The handle was a dark and heavy wood. Anitta picked it up and saw her reflection on the blade, sparkling in the fading light of the late-afternoon sun.

Where was she? What was happening?

She tucked the knife behind her belt and entered the city.

She heard voices coming from a building, sounding like a restaurant or a bar.

She hesitated for a moment, then pushed the oval doors and stepped inside.

It was a bar, with chairs, tables, guests, food and drinks. People were chatting and laughing, not too many, but enough to fill the space.

All eyes turned to Anitta.

Silence.

She walked to the bar and faced the bartender. Then she realized what was terribly wrong…

These people had three eyes,…all of them…

And they were all staring at her, because she had only two…

Maybe she had gone crazy and lost her memory and escaped from some asylum…

"Hey, bartender, can I have something fizzy and cold to drink, like coke zero or something?" she whispered in panic, under the three-eyed gaze of the alien.

They stared at each other.

The bartender replied in a language that vaguely resembled English, but she could hardly understand a word.

Anitta realized she would have to use gestures and motioned that she wanted to drink, that she was thirsty.

The man behind the bar seemed to get it and poured a cherry-coloured drink from a colourful machine into a glass made of blue translucent crystal. He made something on his face that looked like a smile and slid the glass over to Anitta.

She was unsure, because what if this was good for them but poisonous for her?

She hesitated a little more, then climbed onto a high chair made of silver metal.

She observed the man who served her the cherry drink and noticed some more strange things. It was hard to tell if he was male or female. His teeth were very sharp, like shark teeth. His skin was slightly purple and his eyes were fluorescent green. He looked tough, like a warrior from another galaxy.

More guests - aliens came closer to inspect Anitta.

One hand touched her hand. It had six fingers with sharp claws.

The alien's skin was honey-coloured and scaly and very warm.

She pulled her hand back and felt someone touching her hair. She heard voices of admiration, she felt the atmosphere…

She had felt the same way when she first came to America.

But this was on a different level…

There was only one way to adapt to the new situation: Jump into the water and swim with sharks!

She lifted the aqua marine blue crystal glass and the aliens - or rather, the locals, since she was the alien here - watched her and waited for her reaction. It felt like someone watching you taste the food or drink they made for you.

Anitta noticed that and felt a strange sense of comfort - as if she had just returned home after years of isolation from her community.

She raised the glass and touched the liquid with her tongue.

Then she took a sip, and another, and another, because it was so good, so refreshing.

It tasted like a mix of coke and cherry juice, with a hint of blood, vanilla and blueberries. She smiled at the locals and gave them a thumbs up to show her appreciation.

The odd beings seemed pleased by that and resumed their loud conversations.

Anitta said: "It's good!"

She tried to use gestures and smiles to be friendly, she was in survival mode.

Some of the locals invited her to join them at their table.

Another guest came with a box and joined the table where Anitta sat.

Everyone was curious about Anitta, maybe they realized she was a stranger to this place and they showed a lot of empathy towards her.

The three-eyed guest opened the box and took out some beautiful crystals.

Everyone around the table gasped at the beauty of the mineral.

The newcomer took out another crystal and put it in front of Anitta, then pointed with his claw at her eyes, wondering and saying something to the others.

It was a stunning yellow crystal, perfectly shaped and translucent.

Anitta looked around and saw that all the guests had different crystals of various shapes and colours on their tables.

She felt a sudden need to go to the bathroom, and also a bit dizzy - probably from the drink.

She gestured that she would be back soon and her new friends nodded.

She grabbed her suitcase and left the table, looking for the restroom or something like it.

As she walked down the corridor, she wondered: "Where will I sleep tonight?"

Anitta found a room that looked like a bathroom, with cubicles and all…

Good, at least something was familiar or similar…

Anitta went to the mirror and said to herself "God, let it be just a dream, please!"

She closed her eyes and repeated this mantra over and over.

It must have taken ages.

She felt like a Buddhist monk somewhere up in the Himalayas.

"God, let it be just a dream, please!"

She placed a suitcase onto the marble sink and using the knife she found she managed to open it.

There was a big yellow envelope inside with a note: *"Instructions for Anitta"*…

She opened the envelope and pulled a plain white A4 paper, pencil and eraser.

Then there was an another paper with the instructions.

It was an english language test.

Anitta opened her eyes realizing she is in a classroom full of pupils.

"…while our dear Anitta is sleeping once again,…what was Anitta doing last night?"

teacher asked sarcastically.

"Just calm down, you freak!" she just replied laughing into teacher's face.

"You're the best!" said a boy sitting right behind Anitta.

"Sure I am!" she snapped.

Introduction to Hypnosis by Heinrich Cristian Columbus

In the land of the Nibelungen, a young dwarf named Alberich worked as a blacksmith. One day, he heard a sound from the river and saw the Rhinemaidens. They were lovely beings who guarded a ring of gold. The ring had the power to rule the world.

Alberich wanted the ring for himself and snatched it from the Rhinemaidens. They were angry and tried to catch him, but he was too quick and got away.

Alberich wore the ring and felt its power. He became unstoppable and could command the elements. But the ring also changed him. He became cruel and greedy and used the ring to harm others.

In the end, Alberich's greed and power brought him doom. He was tricked by his own kin and was slain. The ring was gone, but its power still haunted the land.

The Ring of the Nibelungen is a warning about the perils of power. It's a story about how it can spoil even the good ones. It is also a story of how the quest for power can lead to ruin.

***

It was a crisp autumn day in the forests of Moravia. A group of influential Nazis - army officers, doctors, scientists, ideologues, industrialists, and agitators - had gathered for a hunting expedition. They split up into smaller groups, some on foot and some on horseback, following the eager dogs that sniffed for prey. The colourful woods seemed to invite them to enjoy the hunt in the midst of nature.

The year was 1936 - the year of the Munich Olympics.

Back then, the *Jeseniky Mountains* in Moravia were still part of Czechoslovakia. The country was a democracy, but it faced the threat of Nazi Germany.

Nazi agents and militants were active in *Jeseniky Mountains* in Moravia in the 1930s. They stirred up trouble by spreading Nazi propaganda and recruiting people to their cause. They also committed sabotage and violence against the Czech government and its allies.

Nazi agents and militants in Jesenik were part of a larger network of Nazi operations in Czechoslovakia. The Nazis wanted to weaken the country and make it easier for Germany to take over. They also wanted to spread their ideology and gain new followers.

The Czech government knew about Nazi activity in Jesenik and tried to stop it. They increased security in the area and arrested suspected Nazi agents. They also intervened against Nazi propaganda and actions.

Nazi activity in Jesenik was a big challenge for the Czech government. They realised that the Nazis wanted to destabilise the country and that they could pose a serious danger to the Czech people. The government fought back against Nazi activity, but they couldn't stop it completely. The Nazis managed to create problems in *Jeseniky Mountains* and succeeded in spreading their ideology and gaining new followers.

But today, they didn't care about problems. It was a beautiful November day, and they were hunting.

One of the small groups included Heinrich Cristian Columbus, a scientist-psychiatrist from Bayreuth who had moved with his wife and children to *Jeseniky Mountains* in Sobotin.

He was a very educated man who had graduated from several universities. He was also a member of the secret society *Six Fingered Hands*, which was basically a small branch of the secret organisation *Illuminati*, which was founded in Bavaria in 1776. The Illuminati was founded by Adam Weishaupt, a professor of law at the University of Ingolstadt. The goal of the Illuminati was to create a new world order based on reason and science. The organisation was disbanded in 1785, but it has been the subject of much speculation and conspiracy theories ever since.

✱ ✱ ✱

Heinrich rode his horse with a rifle on his shoulder and a hunting cap tilted to the side. He also wore a pheasant feather on his cap, as was customary.

He looked young for his age, but he was not as innocent as he seemed. He was already on his sixth cross.

He had black hair and a moustache. He had a strong build and a cheerful smile.

He was a successful man in every way. He had three children and a loving wife. He liked to sneak out at night and go to Brno to join the congregation of *Six Fingered Hands* on his motorcycle or in his car.

Heinrich was a talented scientist and a brilliant psychiatrist.

With Heinrich, there were also Dr. Bruno Hugo, a stout heart surgeon from the Prague Hospital, and his grandson Sigfried Hugo.

Siegfried Hugo liked to wear sailor's striped T-shirts and different glasses. He liked sunglasses, motorcycle glasses, and other kinds. His dream was to travel around the world on a motorcycle or on a boat.

He liked adventure, he was good with women, he was athletic, and he always had that confident playboy smile on his face.

He was a medical student, like his grandfather Bruno.

His grandmother Hilda liked to cook for him, because he enjoyed her food very much. He especially liked Czech donuts with apricot jam or noodles with butter, sugar and grind poppy seeds.

But he also fancied a hearty German-style pork schnitzel covering the plate with baked potatoes, and a mug of Czech beer.

He liked to wear beads made of semi-precious stones on his wrists, which Uncle Heinrich got for him from the half-Jewish merchant Cyril Cilek, who had a shop on the square in the city of Jesenik.

He learned from Heinrich that the merchant Cilek was not doing well, and that he had a large family - a lot of hungry mouths, and that Uncle Heinrich simply bought the jewels, necklaces and rings out of charitable motives.

However, one thing should be said, namely that Mr. Cyril gave extra value to his products.

He knew, for example, what kind of stone brings good to a person, that, for example, the "Tiger's Eye" shields its owner from the evil intentions of others and from their envy, or that

"Chrysoberyl" has the power to foresee the future, brings the owner self-confidence, a tendency to forgive, understand others.

And that pleased Uncle Heinrich and his nephew Siegfried very much.

And so Cilek not only bought stones and jewellery, but also wore them.

If it weren't for them, Cyril's family would probably perish from hunger.

In addition, the Cilek had a house on the edge of town, near the forest, under a hill, and they had to heat a lot, because the *Jeseniky Mountains* were and are a harsh region.

A beautiful region, but full of poor people - the Germans mostly owned farms and the Czechs worked tirelessly on them.

This region essentially belonged to the Germans, even though it was part of Czechoslovakia - however, Czechs and Germans got along quite well.

But Hitler and the fifth column had other - devilish plans.

It was approaching rough times.

* * *

The group became somewhat isolated from the rest - they didn't even hunt much - rather they roamed through the forest on horseback - they stopped here and there, had something to eat, enjoyed a cigarette or schnapps and discussed everyday and scientific matters, politics and history, as well as what it might bring future.

Heinrich recoiled as he ventured deeper into the forest, where a hidden trail of moss-covered rocks beckoned him. He left his companions to their picnic and followed his curiosity, winding through a narrow ravine. Suddenly, a sharp pain stabbed his lower back and a wave of nausea washed over him.

He collapsed on the ground and propped himself against a pine tree, inhaling its fragrant resin. Pine needles jabbed his rear, but he barely noticed. His head spun and his energy drained. He reached for a bottle of schnapps and gulped it down. Then he drank some water from his hunter's flask and broke off a piece of chocolate. He hoped he didn't have diabetes, he was too young for that…

He fished out a silver case from his hunting coat and snapped it open. He picked one cigarette from the neatly arranged row and tucked it in his mouth. The silver case, adorned with intricate patterns, snapped shut and disappeared. He struck a match and lit his cigarette. He took a deep drag and closed his eyes.

Suddenly, he heard a strange noise - like rocks tumbling down, or someone hitting the marble floor with an oak staff - and the echoes reverberated off the walls.

Heinrich exhaled the smoke and opened his eyes.

He gasped in terror!

A figure stood before him. The figure was tall and thin, with long white hair and a beard. He wore a long black robe.

Heinrich asked, "Who are you?"

The figure replied, "I am Alberich, the spirit of a dwarf who once owned the ring of the Nibelungs."

"The ring of the Nibelungs?" Heinrich echoed. "I know of it. It's a magic ring that grants its bearer dominion over the world."

"That is so," Alberich said. "But it is also a doomed ring. It will only bring woe and misery to its bearer."

"What do you want from me?" Heinrich asked.

"I want you to take the ring," Alberich said. "I want you to wield its power to aid people."

"But I don't want the ring," Heinrich said. "I don't want to be doomed."

"You don't have to be doomed," Alberich said. "You can use the ring for good. You can use it to help people."

Heinrich pondered Alberich's words. He knew the ring was a potent artefact and knew it could be used for good or evil. He also knew that Alberich was right about the doom. The ring would bring him nothing but trouble and sorrow. But he also knew that he could help people with the ring.

"I'll take the ring," Heinrich said.

"Good," Alberich said. "You won't regret it."

Alberich reached into his robes and produced a ring. He gave it to Heinrich. Heinrich took the ring and slipped it on his finger.

"Thank you," Heinrich said.

"You're welcome," Alberich said. "Now go and use the ring for good."

Alberich disappeared. Heinrich watched him go, then headed back to his friends.

He felt he had made the right choice. He would use the ring to help people. He would use it to improve the world.

But then he paused and burst into laughter at the ridiculousness of the whole situation, but he was looking at the ring.

"Probably some lunatic," he muttered to himself.

However, as he examined the gift, it looked like real gold, so he decided to go to a jeweller and a collector of gems - his friend - a half-Jewish, a dealer Cyril.

He asks him what he thinks of it, whether it is gold or not.

Cyril Cilek was from Ostrava and moved to Jesenik for the geological sites. He was a collector of minerals.

He also brought his large family with him - he had many children and little money.

He tried to sell stones in a small shop he opened in the center of Jesenik.

Cyril knew Heinrich because he occasionally came to buy some jewellery.

Not that he needed it when he was already buying a gift - then he was buying gold, diamonds.

But he enjoyed chatting with Cyril in his broken Czech.

* * *

Heinrich entered Cyril's shop and glanced around. It was a small place with shelves of minerals and jewellery. Cyril was behind the counter, buffing a piece of amber.

"Hello, Heinrich," Cyril greeted him. "What brings you here today?"

"I have something I want you to see," Heinrich said. He dug into his pocket and produced a ring. "I found it in the forest."

Cyril took the ring and inspected it. "It's a lovely ring," he said. "But it's not gold."

"It isn't?" Heinrich asked.

"No," Cyril said. "It's a different metal, something I've never seen before."

"What do you think it is?" Heinrich asked.

"I don't know," Cyril said. "But it must be worth a lot."

"How much?" Heinrich asked.

"I don't know," Cyril said. "But I'm sure you could get a good deal for it."

"I'm not looking to sell it," Heinrich said. "I want to know what it is."

"I don't know if I can help you with that," Cyril said. "But I can tell you it's a very powerful ring."

"Powerful?" Heinrich asked. "How?"

"It is said that the ring can give its owner dominion over the world," Cyril said.

"That's absurd," Heinrich said.

"Maybe," Cyril replied. "But it's a legend that has been around for ages."

"I don't care about legends," Heinrich remarked.

"Maybe you should," Cyril whispered. "Because that ring is not to be messed with."

Heinrich looked at the ring. He didn't know what to think. *Was it really a potent ring? Or was it just a myth that everyone wanted to believe?*

He said, "I'll keep it. I'll find out what it is."

"Be careful," Cyril warned him. "That ring could be perilous."

"I'll be careful," Heinrich said.

He wore the ring on his finger and gazed at it. He didn't know what to think of it. *Was it really a powerful ring? Or was it just a foolish legend?*

He decided to keep the ring. He would discover what it is and what it can do.

"How are things with you, my dear friend? How is the family, the wife, the children?" Heinrich asked Cyril with genuine interest.

Cyril just shrugged. "Don't ask, no glory…" he said.

"What's troubling you, confide in your friend, the friend who happens to be also a psychologist…" Heinrich urged.

"Nothing special, it's just that I don't enjoy anything lately, I'm always tired, I want to sleep, but I can't sleep…" Cyril said irritably and put on a small magnifying glass to his eye to inspect a single green crystal in the stone.

Heinrich stroked his moustache and because he was curious by nature and liked to solve things he leaned towards Cyril. "Why can't you sleep, what's happening?"

"Thoughts haunt me…I even hear voices…" Cyril said softly, as if he was afraid that someone would overhear him.

Heinrich raised his eyebrows. "Voices?" he asked. "What voices?"

Cyril looked up from the crystal he was studying. "I don't know," he said. "They're just…there. They talk to me. They tell me things."

Heinrich asked, "What things?"

"They tell me to do something," Cyril said. "They tell me to hurt people."

Heinrich's eyes widened. "You need to see a doctor," he said. "This is serious."

"I know," Cyril said. "I've been trying to get an appointment, but the wait is long."

"Until then," Heinrich said, "you need to avoid sharp objects. And you need to tell someone you trust what's going on."

"I will," Cyril said. "I promise."

Heinrich put his hand on Cyril's shoulder. "I'm here for you," he said. "You're not alone."

Cyril nodded. "Thank you," he said. "I appreciate that."

Heinrich left Cyril's shop, concerned about his friend. He knew that Cyril was a good person, but he also knew that he was in trouble. He hoped that Cyril would be able to get the help he needed.

✳ ✳ ✳

A few days later Heinrich got a call from Cyril. "I'm in the hospital," Cyril said. "I tried to hurt myself."

Heinrich was stunned. "What happened?" he asked.

"I couldn't sleep," Cyril said. "The voices were telling me to hurt people. I couldn't resist them."

Heinrich felt a surge of sadness and anger. "I'm so sorry," he said. "I wish I could help you."

"You did help me," Cyril said. "You told me to go to the doctor. If I hadn't listened to you, I might be dead now."

Heinrich was relieved to hear that Cyril was still alive. "I'm glad you're okay," he said.

"I'm not okay," Cyril said. "I'm afraid. I don't know what will happen to me."

"You'll be okay," Heinrich said. "You're in the hospital now. You'll get the help you need."

"I hope so," Cyril said.

Heinrich talked with Cyril on the phone for a while, trying to reassure him. He told Cyril that he was there for him and that he would support him through this.

Heinrich invited Cyril to his office for a hypnosis session. He wanted to see if he could help Cyril find the cause of his insomnia and hallucinations.

* * *

Cyril came to Heinrich's office anxious and wary. He had never been hypnotised before and didn't know what to expect.

Heinrich calmed Cyril down by explaining the procedure of hypnosis and answering his questions.

Cyril settled in the couch.

Psychiatrist Heinrich was sitting beside him in his big chair.

"Are you ready, mate?" Heinrich asked.

"Yes," Cyril said.

The room was dark except for the flickering light of the fireplace.

Rain poured from the sky and thunder roared outside.

The only other sound was the ticking of the antique clock above the fireplace.

Psychiatrist started hypnosis.

Heinrich began with asking Cyril to focus on his breathing. He told Cyril to breathe deeply and slowly, and then asked him to empty his mind of all thoughts.

"You are sitting in a cozy chair, your feet are on the footstool.

You are relaxed and at ease. The sound of rain and the ticking of the clock soothes you to sleep.

You close your eyes and let your mind wander. You forget all the things that trouble you.

You forget about your work, relationships, finances. You let go of all these worries and let them drift away.

You concentrate on your breath. You breathe slowly and deeply. You feel your body relax.

You feel yourself sinking into the chair. You feel your muscles loosen up. You feel your mind go blank.

You are calm,…you are relaxed,…you are asleep," Heinrich spoke to the patient Cyril in a soothing voice.

The rain keeps falling outside. The thunder keeps rumbling. The clock keeps ticking.

After a few minutes, Heinrich began to speak in a gentle, soothing voice. He told Cyril that he would count down from ten and that when he reached zero Cyril would be in a deep state of hypnosis.

Heinrich counted down from ten, and as he did Cyril felt himself relax more and more. When Heinrich reached zero, Cyril was in a deep state of hypnosis.

Heinrich then started asking Cyril questions about his insomnia and hallucinations. Cyril was able to answer Heinrich's questions without any difficulty.

Heinrich learned that Cyril's insomnia and hallucinations were caused by a traumatic event that happened in Cyril's childhood. Heinrich also learned that Cyril had suppressed the traumatic event for many years.

When Cyril was a child, he was beaten by his father. His father was a violent man who often hit Cyril and his mother. Cyril's mother was unable to protect him and she was also abused by Cyril's father.

Heinrich put his hand on Cyril's head:

"You are asleep. You are calm. You are relaxed."

You hear the piano playing softly and all your problems melt away into a magical melody like notes in the air of the enchanted gardens of the castle at the foot of the mountain with a beautiful view of the valley with lindens and oaks, with apple trees and rose-hip bushes, the grasses sway in the gentle spring breeze that whispers - welcome home - to paradise - Cyril - here is eternity - endless youth, health and love - here you belong.

So come and join us - we're all on the terrace - it's time for lunch together."

***

Cyril drifted off, or rather drifted into a hypnotic state.

Meanwhile, Heinrich moved to the piano and softly - just lightly - played Mozart's "Rondo alla Turca".

It was raining outside and the drops hit the window panes between notes and there was thunder now and then.

Flashes lit up the room with the fireplace, in which the fire was burning and crackling like a horse.

The crowns of the trees out there swayed in the gusts of wind, and the Melusine let out drawn-out wailing sounds.

But they were not unpleasant, on the contrary.

***

Cyril blinked and saw the clear blue sky and the dark eyes of a stunning girl.

Her raven hair with a violet tint danced in the gentle wind.

They were lying on a grassy field full of cheerful people having a picnic.

Cyril felt a moment of confusion, but then he propped himself up and rubbed his eyes - he gazed at the lovely creature and grinned.

Cyril stretched his arms, let out a drowsy yawn, and scanned his surroundings. He was in a gorgeous field, among people having a picnic. The sun was bright, the birds were chirping and the air was fragrant with flowers. He felt happy and calm.

He glanced at the girl beside him. She beamed at him and said, "Welcome to paradise, Cyril."

Cyril beamed back at her. "Thank you," he said. "It's beautiful."

"I'm happy you like it here," said the girl. "This is where I live.

"Where you live?" Cyril asked. "But how can that be?"

"It's all about how you see things," said the girl. "This is my world and you can stay here as long as you wish.

Cyril looked around again. He saw that everyone in the field was blissful and satisfied. He really felt like he could stay here forever.

"Thank you," he said again. "I want to stay.

The girl smiled. "I'm glad," she said. "Then let's have some food."

The girl got up and offered Cyril her hand. He took her hand and together they strolled to the picnic table.

As they ate, Cyril learned that the girl's name was Anya. She told him that she was a nymph and that she had dwelled in the field for ages. She told him about the other beings that lived in the field, about the flora and fauna that thrived there.

Cyril listened to Anya's tales with keen interest. He felt like he had finally found a place where he fit in.

After they ate, Anya took Cyril for a walk in the field. She showed him her favourite spots and they talked about their hopes and dreams.

Cyril felt as if he had known Anya all his life. He felt like he could share anything with her.

As the sun started to sink, Anya led Cyril back to the picnic table.

"I have to leave now," she said. "But I'll come back tomorrow."

"I'll wait for you," said Cyril.

Anya smiled and kissed Cyril on the cheek. Then she turned and walked away, vanishing into the woods.

*** * ***

Cyril lingered at the picnic table, soaking in the last rays of the sun. He felt a warm glow of happiness and gratitude. He would always cherish his memories of Anya, and he knew she would always welcome him back to her meadow.

But as the sky turned from orange to purple, Cyril realised he had nowhere to sleep.

He got up and wandered along the forest path, looking for a shelter. The night fell quickly, and soon he was surrounded by darkness.

He quickened his steps, trying to recall where he came from.

The path became steeper and rockier, and he heard eerie noises from the woods.

Wolves howled, owls hooted, and other mysterious creatures stirred in the shadows.

Cyril muttered to himself, *"If I can reach the top, maybe I'll see some lights, a castle, a church, or a village. Maybe I'll know where to go next. Maybe I'll even remember who I am and where I belong."*

And with that hope, the man hastened his climb.

Cyril came across an old man on the path. The man wore a long black cloak that hid his body and a hood that shadowed his face.

In his hand, he carried a wooden walking stick with a devil's head on top. The devil had horns and ruby eyes that glowed red.

Cyril felt a surge of fear.

He stopped in his tracks and stared at the old man. The man was tall and lean, his cloak billowing in the wind. His hood was low over his eyes, but Cyril could see them shining red.

A cold shiver ran through Cyril. He had never encountered anything like this before. He didn't know how to react.

The old man pointed his walking stick at Cyril. "Who are you?" he demanded in a deep, thundering voice.

Cyril was too scared to speak. He just gaped at the old man with his mouth open.

"Speak up!" the old man shouted. "Who are you?"

Cyril managed to say something. "I…I'm Cyril," he said.

"Cyril?" the old man repeated. "That's a strange name."

"That's what I'm called," Cyril said.

"Where do you come from, Cyril?" the old man asked.

"I…I don't know," Cyril said. "I can't remember."

"You can't remember?" the old man asked. "How can that be?"

"I don't know," Cyril said. "I just can't remember.

The old man lowered his walking stick. "Interesting," he said. "I can help you."

"You can?" Cyril asked.

"Yes," the old man said. "But first you have to do something for me.

"What is it?" Cyril asked.

"You have to come with me," the old man said.

"Where?" Cyril asked.

"To my castle," the old man said. "It's not far from here.

Cyril hesitated. He didn't know if he should trust the man. But he had no other option.

"Okay," he said. "I'll go with you."

The old man grinned. "Good," he said. "Follow me."

The old man turned and walked away. Cyril followed him, his heart pounding in his chest.

* * *

They climbed the hill and Cyril saw a dreadful castle on the other mountain. It towered over the trees, bathed in the cold light of the full moon.

Bats flitted among the pine and larch branches, and the wolves' howls sounded closer and closer.

"We'll stay here for a bit," the old man snarled and banged his staff on a rock three times. It made a loud thunder-like noise.

Soon, Cyril heard the horses' neighs, the driver's yell, the wagon's squeak, and the carriage's wheels.

It burst out of the forest and raced towards them.

The carriage was black as night, the horses were black as coal, and the driver was black as death.

His face was a horror. Cyril saw two dark pits in a white skull glaring at him.

"Good day, my lord," the driver said in a raspy voice, clacking his teeth and bowing slightly.

***

Cyril was petrified. He had never encountered anything like the ghostly charioteer before. He didn't know how to react.

The old man spoke to the driver. "Take us to my castle," he said.

The charioteer nodded and whipped his horse. The carriage jerked forward and Cyril was pushed back into the seat.

The carriage flew through the forest, the horses' hooves pounding and rattling on the earth. Cyril clung to the seat as the carriage swerved and bounced.

At last the carriage stopped in front of a huge black castle with many spires. The old man stepped out of the carriage and turned to Cyril.

"This is my home," he said. "You will stay here with me.

Cyril didn't know what to answer. He just nodded and followed the old man into the castle.

The inside of the castle was as dark and gloomy as the outside. The old man took Cyril down a long hall into a big room.

"This is your room," he said. "You will sleep here tonight.

Cyril glanced around the room. It was small and plain, with only a bed and a chest.

"Thank you," he said.

The old man nodded. "I'll leave you alone," he said. "Dinner will be ready in an hour.

The old man exited the room and Cyril was by himself. He sat down on the bed and tried to make sense of everything that had happened. He didn't know where he was or why he was here. But he knew he had to find a way to get away.

There was only a tiny barred window in the corner of the room.

It's going to be tough to escape from here.

"But nothing is impossible," a mysterious voice whispered from nowhere.

Cyril looked around, but saw no one.

Maybe it's not a hallucination, he thought.

"You just have to solve the three riddles the Dark Lord will ask you," a sweet tinkling girl's voice whispered.

Cyril recognised it as Anya - the charming nymph of the flower valley!

"Anya, where are you?" Cyril cried out with excitement and hope in his voice.

He checked under the bed, then quickly in the chest - to see if Anya was hiding there, but there was no one.

Cyril was truly alone in the room.

Then he dragged his bed to the window, climbed onto the bed and stood on his toes.

He peered out the window.

In the opposite tower there was a light in the window, and in that window he saw a face - it was her - Anya!

"Anya, what are you doing there," Cyril thought, because he assumed that Anya wouldn't hear him anyway - even if he shouted - the tower was on the other side on another hill.

But to his surprise, Anya replied "The Dark Lord captured me and locked me in a dark tower at the very top, where vultures and crows come to feed every time there is a full moon and that will be

in three days - at the Tower of Silence!"

"I will rescue you, Anya!" Cyril thought.

"What three riddles?" he asked in his mind.

But Anya could hear him because they were both on the same wavelength and communicating telepathically.

"When you go to dinner - you'll find out," the girl whispered in Cyril's head.

* * *

Cyril felt a surge of relief when he heard Anya's voice, even if it was only in his mind. He knew that as long as she was alive, he had to find a way to rescue her.

He sat on the bed and tried to think of a plan. He knew that the Dark Lord was a mighty wizard and that it would not be easy to beat him. But Cyril was resolved to save Anya, no matter the price.

After a few minutes, Cyril had a plan. He knew that the Dark Lord would anticipate him to try to escape, so he would have to be very sneaky. He will have to wait for the right time to act.

Dinner was ready in an hour and Cyril ate fast. He knew he would need his energy if he wanted to escape. After dinner, the Dark Lord took Cyril into the grand room.

"You will sleep here," said the Dark Lord. "I'll give you three riddles. If you can solve them, you'll be free to leave. But if you fail, you'll be my slave for the rest of your life."

Cyril nodded. He knew the Dark Lord was challenging him and he was determined to win.

The Dark Lord started asking Cyril's riddles. The first one was easy and Cyril answered it right. The second one was harder, but Cyril still managed to answer it.

The third one was the toughest of all. Cyril thought for a long time, but could not figure out an answer.

"I give up," said Cyril. "I don't know the answer to your riddle.

The dark lord grinned. "I knew you wouldn't be able to solve that," he said. "You are mine now.

Cyril was taken to a cell in the dungeon. He was locked in and he knew he would never get out.

But Cyril did not lose hope. He knew Anya was still alive and was resolved to find a way to rescue her.

But he only had three days and three nights. Anya was in grave danger, as vicious hungry vultures and crows would fly in during the full moon, and gruesome gory feasts would happen in the Tower of Silence.

Cyril, however, was tightly bound in shackles and wrapped in chains.

Well, he's no Houdini…

How will he do that?!

***

For two days and two nights, he and Anya talked telepathically about,…well, those things that lovers talk about.

But then the night of doom would come…

Cyril - weakened by hunger and thirst - slumped in his shackles, trying to wet his dry lips with his tongue.

When three light beings appeared before him.

One was of average height, in a suit and with a briefcase in his hand, next to him was a chubby man in a coat and with a red rose in his buttonhole, and the third was a tall young man in a striped sailor outfit.

The young man was smiling, wearing sunglasses and a dreamy look on his face.

All three figures shone with a yellow-orange phosphorescent light.

"Who are you?" Cyril shouted with the last of his energy.

"We have come to free you, Cyril," replied the chubby man and chuckled.

"We have to save Anya!" Cyril whispered.

The average-height man came closer, knelt down and opened the briefcase.

He took out a syringe and rummaged through glass bottles of chemicals.

Cyril noticed that the man - or rather a ghost - had a moustache under his nose - he remembered someone suddenly, but he still had to dig deeper in his memory.

The light being filled the syringe with a liquid and injected it into the large rusty lock that held Cyril in shackles.

The lock began to smoke and some foul-smelling green phosphorescent liquid dripped out of it.

The ethereal being waited for a moment, then the stout fellow with the red rose on his buttonhole handed him a big hammer.

The saviour hit the lock, once, twice, and the third time the lock broke into tiny pieces.

Cyril was free, but as he was completely exhausted, he immediately fell to the floor until his eyes closed and the light beings vanished.

He didn't even have time to thank his mysterious saviours, he just muttered "Anya".

The last thing he heard was her longing song from afar - from the Tower of Silence.

***

"Sir?"

"Can you hear me?"

"Sir!"

"Come on, wake up!"

Cyril opened his eyes and felt someone slap his cheek.

He saw around him faintly.

Everything was in a kind of blurry fog.

Everything was white.

"Where, where am I?" Cyril whispered with great difficulty and almost fainted.

He felt nauseous and extremely hungry.

His eye-sight was slowly coming back.

Some figures were standing around, he looked at his hand - he had a needle in it and a clear liquid was flowing into his vein through a plastic tube.

There were three men and they were wearing white coats.

He recognised the average-height man - it was his friend Heinrich!

And those next to…those next to him were obviously doctors…the chubby one…that's what he saw in his dream…he had a red rose in his buttonhole and he still has it there now…and next to him…the tall young man - only now he was wearing normal glasses.

Heinrich smiled at Cyril "Thank God!".

Then another doctor came into the room - he was Japanese - holding papers in his hand and a stethoscope around his neck.

The Asian man approached Cyril and gave him a friendly nod.

But he wasn't smiling.

And this contrast caused a surge of anxiety in Cyril.

✼ ✼ ✼

Heinrich and Cyril strolled slowly through the March garden in the morning, and the first birds had already started to sing louder.

It was still chilly, but the sun was already getting stronger and warmed their backs.

Heinrich gestured Cyril to sit on the bench.

"I have something important to tell you, Cyril.

"It won't be easy for you…" he added.

"What do you mean…" Heinrich looked gravely at his friend and couldn't go on.

But then he took a breath as he gathered his nerve.

"Well, we just, um, the hypnosis went a little wrong…" he said.

"Did I faint? Did I black out? What happened? And what about…Anya! My God, what day is it today? Is there a full moon tonight?" Cyril suddenly bombarded his friend Heinrich with questions.

Heinrich, with a moustache under his nose and with dimples on his cheeks, shook his head.

"You were sleeping, Cyril, we couldn't wake you up, we had to take you to the hospital here in Prague, you slept for a long time…".

"How long? That can't be true. I have to go back right away! For Anya. Do you understand?"

Heinrich looked at his friend bewilderedly and then looked away "You slept for two years, more than two years…".

"I'm so sorry Cyril, it's probably my fault."

Cyril saw another patient holding a newspaper.

He jumped from the bench, ran to the patient and grabbed the newspaper from his hands.

A photo of Adolf Hitler and the headline "The German army invaded Czechoslovakia today!" immediately hit him in the eye.

Then he noticed the date of the newspaper "March 15, 1939".

Cyril stared at Heinrich, only now noticing that his friend was wearing a German uniform.

Heinrich just smiled sadly and made a gesture as if he was innocent.

Cyril stared at Heinrich, only now grasping how much time had gone by.

He slept for two years and during that time the world changed dramatically. The Nazis occupied Czechoslovakia and the world was on the edge of war.

Cyril knew he had to find Anya, but he also knew it would be hard.

The Nazis were everywhere and would hunt down anyone who would resist them. But Cyril was resolved to find Anya, no matter the price.

He turned to Heinrich. "I have to go," he said.

But then he stopped "And what about my wife and children,…in Jesenik?"

He jumped up to Heinrich and shook him by the shoulders "Are they okay? Heinrich!"

Heinrich shook his head sadly and silently.

Then he said softly "You know, the Jews are suffering right now…"

"Where are they, speak, Heinrich, just speak!"

"There was a fire in your house and,…" Heinrich couldn't finish the sentence and a tear rolled down his face.

Then he shook his head and stood up looking at Cyril curled up on the bench.

"No one survived, I'm sorry, they were fascists, and I'm ashamed to be one of them…such are the times…"

Cyril jumped up and grabbed Heinrich by the neck "You have to put me back - into that hypnosis - I have to save Anya, do you understand?!"

Heinrich looked at Cyril for a moment and then nodded his head.

Cyril buried his face in Heinrich's arms and he stroked his hair.

"I want to stay there - in that hypnosis - forever - I will save Anya and we will be there together forever, you have to do it for me, Heinrich," Cyril sobbed.

Heinrich looked somewhere in the distance and then nodded his head.

"Maybe it will be better for you, friend…" Heinrich whispered.

Cyril pushed Heinrich away and he lit a cigarette, which he took out of the silver case.

It was cold, and Heinrich buttoned the last button of the white coat he wore over his German uniform.

Maybe it wasn't just the cold, maybe Heinrich wanted to hide the uniform, perhaps he realised he was on the side of evil, he was ashamed of himself.

＊＊＊

Heinrich walked Cyril through the dark and damp bunker. The walls were concrete and the floor was covered in dust. The only light came from a few faint bulbs that were hanging from the ceiling.

Cyril heard the sound of the boots of Nazi soldiers in the distance. He knew they were under surveillance and felt nervous.

Heinrich stopped at a door and knocked three times. A moment later the door opened and a Nazi soldier came out.

"Heinrich," said the soldier. "What are you doing here?"

"I came to check the Portal," Heinrich said.

The soldier looked at Cyril. "Who is he?"

"That's Cyril," said Heinrich. "He is the one who will use the Portal.

The soldier nodded. "Very well. Follow me."

The soldier led Heinrich and Cyril down a long hall. The walls were full of doors and Cyril could hear people talking and laughing behind them.

The soldier stopped at a door and opened it. "Here it is," he said.

Cyril entered the room and looked around. The room was small and square and the walls were made of glass. In the center of the room was a big machine. The machine was made of metal and had a bunch of dials and gauges on it.

"This is the Portal," Heinrich said. "It's a device that allows people to travel to other worlds.

Cyril looked at the Portal in awe. He couldn't believe he was about to go through this and travel to another world.

"How does it work?" he asked.

"The portal uses a mix of magic and technology," Heinrich said. "Magic allows people to enter the Portal and technology allows them to travel to other worlds.

"It's amazing," said Cyril.

"Yes, it is," said Heinrich. "But it is also very risky. The portal is not fully stable and there is always the chance that it could fail."

"I understand," said Cyril. "I'm ready to risk it.

"I'm glad to hear that," said Heinrich. "Because Anya is depending on you.

Cyril nodded. "I won't let her down."

Heinrich smiled. "I know you won't. Now take this ring. It is Alberich's Ring of the Nibelung. It is a powerful magical ring that will help you in your quest."

Cyril takes the ring from Heinrich.

Cyril: "Thank you."

Heinrich: "Good luck, Cyril."

Cyril: "Thank you."

Cyril is about to enter the lucid dream portal.

Heinrich: "Cyril!"

Cyril turns around.

Cyril: "Yes?"

Heinrich: "If the ring shows its power, I already know what you will do to the Nazis."

Cyril: "I'll defeat them."

Heinrich: "Okay. I know you'll succeed."

Cyril: "I will."

Heinrich watches him go and knows that Cyril will succeed.

Cyril took a deep breath and walked through the portal. He felt a weird sensation and then he was gone.

Heinrich watched Cyril go and knew he was taking a big gamble. But he also knew that Cyril was the only one who could save Anya.

Heinrich turned to the soldier. "I trust you will keep it a secret?"

The soldier nodded and smiled oddly. "My lips are sealed."

Heinrich smiled sadly, "I know," and with that he pulled out his gun and shot the soldier dead.

He then dragged the body to the portal and shoved it inside until it vanished without a trace.

Heinrich took out his silver case and tapped it with his finger.

"*Well, that's it...*" thought Heinrich as he lit a cigarette with a match.

Nathrengar's Necklace

Better the devil you know, than the devil you don't...

Treasure can mean different things to different people - some think of a chest full of gold, some crave fame of various kinds, some seek ancient wisdom, magic powers, journeys to other worlds, lucid dreams and astral travels. But for many, the ultimate treasure is true love, because deep down, we all have lost love at some point and are still looking for it. Love is the real force and motive behind everything, and without it, there would be nothing - only cold endless void - nothingness - eternal damnation.

Every seeker has to pay a price for the treasure she or he chooses, a price of unimaginable value, and she or he would give anything for it - even her or his life - even the soul. Many have sold their souls to the devil - one could say the majority - because any verbal, mental or even subconscious agreement with the dark forces is recorded and inscribed in Natherngar's Book of Light & Darkness. This agreement is final and everlasting - such a soul will never incarnate again as a human or another intelligent being, but will wander through the infinitely dreadful realm of darkness. Only a few souls will ascend to heaven, where there is love, freedom - where ego has no place - where unity and peace prevail. It is a vast land, full of enchanted gardens, turquoise waterfalls and oases in glittering deserts - where camel caravans travel with loads of delicious food, tea and coffee. There are stalls along the way, where you can enjoy hot mint tea and smoke a "camel" cigarette without risking cancer. In that country, cigarette packs don't have those horrible pictures of suffering people like here on earth. They make the best rosemary grilled chicken here, with poached eggs and big crunchy fries and a fresh vegetable salad with olive oil and apple cider vinegar. You can also have a non-alcoholic beer or lemonade with ice from the glaciers of the *Aquamarine Mountains*. Or you can taste the hot Harira soup with lamb, chickpeas, tomatoes and exotic spices, along with a handful of the finest dates and Chabakyia sweets. You can also try the Msaman pancake with black coffee or an avocado milkshake. The women here have beautiful black hair that reaches the floor and shines with a metallic blue hue, their eyes are big, sparkling and black as coal. Their breasts are large and their bodies are slim, their skin is honey-smooth and tanned and their lips are full and tempting to be kissed. Their voice soothes with its tone and delights with its singing - they are angels. In the cool shade of white houses and their psychedelic-coloured and fragrant gardens, you can daydream or sleep... Here in heaven, you don't have to do anything else - nor do you want to. Those beautiful laughing girls are like Samuel's wife Laura. Because of her and for her, he decided to find his treasure!

Finding any treasure - whatever it may be - is not only very hard, but also very risky. Many treasures have their own guardians, and some of them are better left alone. They are often creatures from worlds so alien to ours - twisted creatures, undead, mutants, wicked beings and spirits - who have no regard for the human quest for wealth and fame. Those worlds can be worse than hell itself, and they have swallowed many a rich man, artist, politician, miner, shopkeeper, lender, fashion designer, detective, garbage collector, gold digger or treasure hunter - forever. Nathrengar waits patiently for his prey, and it can be anyone - a family man who is willing to get into debt with the bank so that his kids can go to prestigious colleges and his wife can have her dream house with a garden - bigger than her childhood friends' for sure - someone who would do things that are immoral and downright abhorrent - beyond human law - just to show off his success in his field at a reunion,…the best car,…wearing an expensive designer shirt,…someone who claims to help the needy,…someone who likes to talk too much,…someone who feeds on admiration and gets high on envy,…someone with an ego as big as the gate to hell itself…

At first there is light, joy and seemingly endless fun - but at the end, there is a dark lord waiting - with the contract signed by the unlucky human…

Samuel Green, a geological engineer and a family man, should have learned about the unsuspectedly huge, cunning and powerful force of evil and darkness.

***

Samuel Green typed an address in North-West Chicago into his sat nav - *the O'Hare airport.* He looked up suddenly when he heard the annoying noise of a helicopter. His eyes in the rearview mirror said: *"This is bad."*

It was night - the night of the ghosts - and the streets were empty - or so it seemed - only some rats scurried across the road - from the trash cans to the warm moist shelter of the sewer.

He drove off.

The car peeled off from the curb and sped down the streets towards the North-West.

A CTR with homeless dwellers flew by above him.

He saw a parked bike painted white with a metal sign that said: *"Father of three, no money, no home, no future - veteran - disabled."*

And below it was written: *"My American Dream"*.

He felt like having some coffee.

Sam stopped at a gas station, got one, in a cup, and his favourite donut to go with it - he felt like a cop.

But he wasn't, not at all.

Samuel Green was on his way to the airport for an adventure in Czech Republic in the heart of Europe and he was pretty excited about it.

* * *

The day is short here, shorter than anywhere else, as if some dark power ruled over the endless impenetrable mysterious forests here. And it should be said that it is not wise to be caught in these forests when the old stars of the night come out. Even during the day, some places here are so desolate, so strangely dreamy and ominously mysterious, that they make the careless wanderer who strays into them feel a cold shiver that he has been drawn here by some creepy monstrous force from other worlds - that he is under its control, and that something terrible is about to happen. That oddly familiar feeling, that *déjà vu*, that he has been here before, and that he keeps coming back again and again for ages. As if everything - all life experiences - were just a prelude to this Ode to Horror played by an orchestra of undeads, witches and creatures whose very sight causes human death by fear.

These mournfully gothic *Jeseniky Mountains* are full of mystical places and dark legends about witches, wizards and their inquisitors or executioners. There are many stories in *Jeseniky* that make the spine tingle about how witches and other unclean forces gathered at the magical Peter stones near the summit of *Praded*. After orgies with the devil, who appeared as a black goat or a cat, they flew back home to harm people in various ways. The tales from the *Jeseniky Mountains* are no less harsh than their vast dark forests and deep gorges where they were born. The people who told them had a need to give shape to evil and good, and so their tales rarely have a kind fairy tale tone. You could say that they are more like a horror movie. One of the reasons why *Jeseniky* legends are grim and merciless is that they are influenced by Germanic mythology. It is more somber and dark than Slavic myths.

In the hollows of forked trees, or in places where various remarkable phenomena happened, supernatural beings dwelled in the forests of *Jeseniky*. There were nymphs, gnomes and permonics, and everything was under the rule of the mighty Great Grandfather. For generations of Jeseniky's mountaineers who mined ore underground or faced the wild nature in the forests of the mountains, these creatures were a source of justice. It is noteworthy that in Jeseniky's legends, evil mostly comes from the side of humans. And that's when those gnomes and nymphs intervene to restore order, they punish the wicked and uphold the law. Where their power is not enough, Grandfather steps in as the highest authority.

In a field near the castle in *Velke Losiny*, there was a tree that was said to remember the execution of the three leaders of the peasant revolt against the authorities in 1662. But the terrible Zerotins family soon outdid themselves with an even bigger horror show, when they sent more than a hundred people to death during the cruel inquisition trials.

All this horror began in 1678. It was an old beggar woman Maria Schuhova, who would do anything for a bit of food, and so she secretly took away a consecrated host from the church on Saturday. She promised it to the Saturday midwife Dorothy, supposedly to make her cow start milking again. A bald one-legged minister with a red goatee and false teeth noticed that the beggar spat out the host into an apricot orange scarf. There were people in the village who liked to talk about things they didn't know. And that man of God - that minister - he immediately ran to report to the parson, who was the biggest gossip in the area and had already caused trouble for more than one talkative person. And the parson, known as a fanatical priest who liked to rant against witches, sent a report to the hands of the estate owner. The strongly Catholic Countess Angelia Anna Sibyl of Galle was of course greatly alarmed by the news of a witch in *Sobotin* and invited Jindrich Frantisek Boblig from Edelstadt, who later became the chairman of the *Losiny* and *Sumperk* inquisition commissions.

✳ ✳ ✳

At the table in the local inn in *Marsikov*, there is only an old man, who sips on his flat warm beer. Behind the bar, there is a young man - maybe a college student - and in the corner by the slot machine, there is a tanned middle-aged man. The TV shows the match of the local soccer league. Just another dull endless autumn afternoon.

They are all startled by a sudden clink of money, heaps of small coins falling down. The old man wakes up from his nap and looks with his glassy tired eyes towards the enticing sound and a faint smile forms on his face. The man at the slot machine takes off his hat, his mouth wide open in a grin - and he grabs a handful of coins from the machine and pours them into his hat.

A young man comes out eagerly from behind the bar: "That's awesome, boss!" *"Maybe he'll tip something from that win…"* he thinks.

The boss looks out the window and sees that it's starting to rain lightly. "Let's close a bit early today and call it a day, maybe We'll have a drink, some homemade apricot brandy and we can roast some sausages, what do you say, kid?" the happy winner shouts and smiles at the bartender.

"Sure thing, boss!"

"Do we still have some stew?"

"Yes, boss."

"Warm up my goulash and get me a beer, and one for yourself too!"

"Sure, great, boss."

"And one for me too!" the old man chimes in from the corner, who until now somehow blended in with the grey peeling wall behind him.

The boss - the owner, or rather the tenant of the inn, hops into the storeroom.

Soon enough, they are all enjoying goulash, sausages and freshly tapped beer. A small bottle with homemade apricot brandy also sits on the table.

Suddenly, the door opened wide with dreadful squeak and a stranger in long black cloak entered room.

The smell of fire and sulfur immediately spread throughout the room.

His long coat was soaked with water for there was a storm raging outside.

He kept a walking stick in one hand and a business suitcase in the other.

He was coughing loudly.

He took a seat in the corner and got rid of his leather gloves throwing them onto the heavy oak table.

When the young waiter approached him, he was dismayed by the sight of the glove, and the boy felt rather uneasy about what he saw...

Was he really counting 6 fingers?

There was something not quite right about the guest...

* * *

Samuel Green was born in Houston, Texas. His parents were both police officers and they wanted little Samuel to follow in their footsteps. Samuel, however, had a passion for collecting minerals and traveling since he was young - so he decided to become a geologist and graduated from college. After school, he got a job at the Museum, where he met his future wife and fathered an astonishing eleven children. Children should be a blessing, but having so many of them in America can be hell, because in America you pay for everything - even a hearty smile - nothing is free in the USA. The salary at the museum was not bad, as Samuel climbed up the career ladder and became the head of the Board of Directors and the Department of Mineralogy, his belly grew and his elbows sharpened. But still, his wife and kids wanted more and more, their bottomless stomachs consumed a lot of food and at school, the kids couldn't have ordinary phones but only the biggest - the most modern - with the most cameras and apps, otherwise they would be mocked by their peers as "losers"! Sam had to buy a mini bus to transport his large family to the weekend shopping spree at the mega super market and to the amusement park - Jesus in heaven - and hot dogs and hamburgers and fries and pizzas and chicken nuggets that are barely edible, and the endless carousel rides, and to the movies, new shoes for his wife, new dresses every month. You can probably imagine Samuel's state of mind... Sam had already taken out a bunch of bank loans and debts... House on mortgage, huge modern brand fridge on credit, mini-bus on credit - everything on credit. And next year, the oldest of his kids are going to college... Samuel often stays at the Museum after work and his head spins over the pile of bills and threatening letters under the dim light of the desk lamp. He often watches the security guard, the old childless lonely black man Ramses - *how he envies him his carefree life* - if only he could - if only he could - he would swap bodies with Ramses - that would be his only way out of this hopeless situation... Ramses seems to sense his envy and dark thoughts, so he tries to avoid any contact with him.

Samuel doesn't know what to make of that fat, even royally obese black man who sits with a slight smile on his face - those spiky glasses with thick lenses - why does he wear them so casually perched on his nose - glasses tilted down as if they could drop to the floor at any moment, if it weren't for those devilishly sharp spikes of his huge ears holding them by the tips of the frame. He could never get a woman like his Laura, let alone keep her! *"Why did they have to breed?"* Samuel thinks. But Samuel is a faithful husband and also very active in sex - and so is his wife. And if we add to that, that Laura - his wife - comes from a conservative family and is strongly opposed to contraception... Plus, Laura is an extremely beautiful and sensual woman. And Samuel loves his Laura very much, he would do anything for her, and he has done a lot already. He calls her his *"Princess"* and Princess Laura doesn't settle for just anyone. Princess Laura only wants Knights! Samuel has to be a knight! Samuel is sitting in his office - the only lit window in the huge museum building - well - one more small window is lit - and that's the window of the security room where the security guard sits - the old man Ramses.

"Maybe I should buy a mask and rob a bank!" Samuel dares himself.

"Anyway, the whole country is in debt and in trouble, and it's only a matter of time before it all explodes..."

"Especially since they keep sending money to Ukraine, Putin will mess it up anyway and they'll fire nuclear missiles at us - he's such an idiot!"

"After all, Samuel was born in America, he thinks he can do and say whatever he wants, then..."

"Well, yeah - but there are also 3 million Americans locked up in prison, and if I don't figure out something soon about those debts,...I might end up there myself..."

Samuel Green turned off the lamp and sat in the Museum engulfed by monstrous darkness for many hours. He finally stopped thinking, his mind stopped working and peace came to his soul. He did what he could. And now he knew exactly what to do…

Samuel had talked to an extremely wealthy gallery owner from downtown yesterday. He asked him to get him a gem - Chrysoberyl - he needed it to cut a stone for a necklace - he would need to find a large enough rough stone, so that he could cut the necessary carats with the necessary quality from it. By chance, Samuel had received a sample of mineral *Chrysoberyl* as a donation from a kid - a gift for the museum from an avid mineralogist - collector.

The sample was interesting, but too small and it came from a site in the Czech Republic from *Marsikov (Marchendorf)* in *Sobotin* in the *Jeseniky Mountains.*

Samuel showed it to the gallery owner and he was mesmerized by its deep green colour - like a crocodile's eye - and its clarity and magical shine, so he decided to pay for Samuel's trip to Europe, so that he could source the necessary rough stone and the necessary size for him, even if he had to search for it at that site himself in person.

Samuel was excited at first, but after doing some research on the internet and sweating bullets, when he called a few well-known geologists in Bohemia, his excitement faded considerably.

The stone - *Chrysoberyl* - is a mineral of considerable brittleness and to cut it to the size that fits into the dream gem, he would need a really big rough stone without cracks. And such stones are very rare, especially those from the *Jeseniky* site in *Bohemia*.

But the gallery owner was stubborn and gave Samuel a substantial advance - to cover the expenses.

He promised Samuel an incredible three million US dollars for the stone!

Such an offer, such a reward, simply can't be turned down. Samuel's chance of finding the required stone in the required size in Czechia is equal to winning the lottery, but even if there is a chance - and Samuel is a skilled geologist, then Samuel has to go and has to try for his family, and also for his pure collector's and professional passion.

Samuel never backed down from a challenge.

Samuel did extensive research on the mineral-gem and he read the following: *Occurrence in the Czech Republic: flat green-yellow crystals (2-3 cm) in Marsikov near Sobotin in Hruby Jesenik in pegmatites. From Marsikov (Marchendorf), from the site Schindelhübel (Rasovna) comes the very first European chrysoberyl. The site was discovered by Mr. Boleslawsky in 1819 and described by Mr. Hruschka in 1824. The wide area around the site is heavily collected nowadays. However, finds are not impossible even today, but the crystals found are rarely bigger than 1 cm.*

This news was not good because Samuel needed to find a much larger crystal - at least 5 x 5 cm, so that he could cut it into a princess' necklace. The princess' code name was *Ruby Delismen Butterfly*, but details like her real name or the country where her father ruled had to be kept strictly secret. Samuel continued - under the light of the art nouveau lamp - diligently with his survey of old books, historical photos, mineralogical magazines or geological studies.

The name "chrysoberyl" comes from the Greek words χρυσός (chrysos) = golden and βήρυλλος (berylos) = beryl, which describe the color of the mineral. Despite the similarity of names - chrysoberyl and beryl are two completely different gems, even though they both contain beryllium. Chrysoberyl is the third hardest commonly found natural gemstone and lies at 8.5 on the Mohs scale of mineral hardness, between corundum (9) and topaz (8). Common chrysoberyl is yellowish green and transparent or translucent. If the mineral has a good light green to yellow colour and is transparent, it is used as a gem.

Identification

Chemical formula: $BeAl_2O_4$

Color: yellow, light green

System: orthorhombic

Hardness: 8.5

Luster: vitreous

Cleavage: good

Streak: white

Density: $3.7\,g\cdot cm{-3}$

Solubility in acids: insoluble

Magical properties: it brings luck, helps to attract attention and favour of others, enhances patience and heals depression, has a positive effect on the heart chakra

Samuel paused at the magical properties and understood why the princess wanted to have chrysoberyl in her necklace - among other precious stones. She was not only beautiful, but also a clever woman. And his eyes fell on the picture of Jesus Christ on the wall touching his red heart, from which dazzling rays of light radiate…

Samuel pondered the topic of light: *"What is it really - the light? And what exactly is darkness? And maybe it's just the human brain - its configuration - the specification of the tool for perceiving, that makes us see things around us… After all, for example, reptiles or flies see things very differently,… feel differently,…perceive,… And what about an eagle! He can spot a small mouse from a great height… And that's not to mention beings from other worlds, artificial intelligence, angels and demons…"*

Samuel's dream last night was unlike any other. He felt everything with a vividness that surpassed his waking life. He sensed a different kind of reality, a paradoxical certainty that he was in a true reality, yet also a surreal one. He felt light and free, as if his soul had no limits. His imagination ran wild, creating fantastical scenes with a feverish and dreamy flair. He felt like he was soaring with the wild geese that flew southward to the warm sea, basking in the gentle sun and resting in the soothing moonlight.

In his dream, he kissed a beautiful girl with long black hair and dark eyes that were kind but stern. She wore a black leather jacket over her arm. He recognized her as Laura, his wife.

Then he entered the grand house that he had visited countless times before. Nothing had changed in the hall. He walked down the corridor and that's when it happened…

The long, spacious corridor with vaulted arches and tiled walls adorned with Arabic frescoes and sandstone bas-reliefs filled him with an intense feeling - that this was the ultimate reality, a reality beyond reason, justification, or purpose, a reality that he always joyfully returned to from all his lives and other strange existences or non-existent eternal voids.

Here and only here was Samuel truly at home, and here and only here his beautiful angel Laura awaited him.

Samuel snapped out of his reverie and came back to our earthly reality.

He searched online for the details of the place where he could find chrysoberyl.

Land registry: Marsikov

Geological region: Silesian rocks and granite mountain

Location: On a hill named Rasovna, 670 m north-northeast from the church in Marsikov

The quaint village of Marsikov lies at the base of the Hruby Jesenik Mountains. It was first mentioned in 1351, when its parish was recorded. There stands an old church dedicated to Saint Michael the Archangel, built in 1609. The village and its surroundings are home to world-renowned mineral deposits. In 1819, the mineral chrysoberyl was discovered here for the first time in Europe, on a trail called "Rasovna" - formerly "Schinderhübel" - by a mineralogist named Boleslawsky.

This is a classic site of beryl-columbite pegmatite, located about 500 meters northeast of the church in Marsíkov, on a hill known as Schinderhübel or Rasovna. The local occurrence of chrysoberyl was first described by Wenzel Hruschka in 1824. A pegmatite vein containing the mineral was found in a cut of the dirt road leading from Marsikov. The vein cuts through amphibole gneisses and is about 50 cm thick. The medium-grained granitic zone consists of albite-oligoclase, quartz, muscovite, garnet, beryl, gahnite, zircon and thin tabular chrysoberyl, which is relatively rare.

*** * ***

Samuel Green, the director of the mineralogical department of the museum in Chicago, had verified this information, but when he drove his old car, bought cheaply at a bazaar in the city of *Karvina* in *Moravia*, to the small village of *Marsikov*, hidden deep in the vast hills, he felt a wave of inexplicable despair wash over him.

Finding the location would not be as easy as he had imagined in his romantic pictures. As he entered the village, he passed by an ancient wooden church with a stone cross bearing Jesus nailed to it. Behind it, on the right side of the road, there was a local inn, where Samuel parked his car.

He sat there for a while and then noticed an old woman and an old man sitting on the opposite side - on the flat roof of a house - peeling potatoes. They both looked up at him. He got out of his car and walked towards them, hoping to ask them for directions to the site, if they knew anything about it.

"Hello, can you please tell me how to get to *Rasovna…*or…*Schinderhübel?*" Samuel asked in broken Czech, glancing at a small English-Czech dictionary.

He had studied Czech diligently before traveling to Moravia in the Czech Republic.

Samuel had a knack for languages, but Czech was a tough one.

The old woman smiled and shook her head.

The old man frowned and eyed the stranger suspiciously.

"What do you want there?" he asked Samuel.

Samuel gave his rehearsed answer: "I collect stones - minerals - and I read that there is *chrysoberyl* on *Schinderhübel.*"

The old man took out a pack of cigarettes and lit one.

"People are always making a big mess there. They dig holes and don't bother to fill them up. A bunch of bastards! Last week, some guys came with an excavator."

"I personally arranged the machine for them - I mean, the rental."

"Well, they paid,…but they could have cleaned up after themselves."

Samuel stepped closer to the old man and reached into his back pocket. He pulled out a green hundred-crown bill and handed it to the man.

"Ugh, sir, *to know where?*" he said in a tragically poor Czech language.

"Hmm, and *young sir have more of these papers?*" the old man mockingly mimicked the foreigner's Czech.

Samuel shook his head as if he didn't understand, but he knew what the old man wanted. The old man snatched the banknote, quickly hid it in his shirt pocket under his coat, and then took a long drag from his cigarette, watching Samuel.

Samuel, with a stingy grin on his face, dug into his pocket again, took out another hundred and gave it to the man with apparent reluctance.

The old man exhaled the smoke he had been holding in his lungs, blowing it in Samuel's face until he coughed and waved his hand before him.

"Okay, young man, listen - you go back to that pub where you parked, you go straight ahead, a little further on there is a bridge on the left,... well, rather a footbridge. You cross that bridge and go up to the apple trees and you reach a field. The field is fenced off,...there is a wire with electric current - be careful,...you go up along it,...watch your moves and don't touch it,...you keep going up towards the forest,...you'll see it,... it's about 500 meters,...then you get to a clearing in the forest,...that's an old trail from sometime in the 19th century,...overgrown,... then you go left on that road,...you walk about 100 meters and you are there."

Samuel didn't catch much - just bits and pieces. The old man took another drag from his cigarette, then tore off a piece of newspaper and drew a simple map for the foreigner. He handed it to him.

Samuel thanked him and smiled at the old couple as he said goodbye. They just nodded and watched him walk away towards his car.

* * *

The sun finally climbed over the hills above *Marsikov* and bathed the valley in golden warmth. The air was filled with the smell of burnt leaves, that came from the fires in the gardens, mingling with the odour of brown-green grass that hid the last traces of another fading summer. Samuel noticed a huge predator flying over the village as he searched the trunk of his car. It was scanning for its prey with its keen eyes, ready to swoop down and sink its sharp talons into the soft fur and carry it away to the tops of the giant spruces, to its nest. There it would peck hungrily at the warm innards and lick the hot blood that steamed in the cold dewy morning of the *Jeseniky Mountains*. The beast probably noticed Samuel too, and if Samuel was smaller - as big as a vole, a squirrel, or a fawn - he might have become another delicious breakfast for the menacing predator whose wingspan seemed so large that it blocked out the sun, casting a dark shadow over Samuel.

Samuel felt a pang in his chest - he missed his family, his country - he was an outsider here, at the mercy of these strangely bleak mountains, this mysteriously gloomy region. He had read a lot about its history, legends, about the burning of witches and wizards, about the cruel and wicked inquisitor Bodlig of Edelstadt, about tortures, about ghost stories, gnomes and fairies, demons and grave monsters.

It was November - pleasantly warm - a gentle breeze tousled his rapidly thinning hair - he had a map to the site - everything was going according to plan, but he still had a feeling that something terrible could happen here, that behind the corners of the old village houses lurked evil, dark brooding sinister beings…

He felt as if he saw, or at least sensed, figures around him - the figures of a ghostly nature - in musty veils - with blurry faces that kept morphing.

He felt the skeletal arms covered in wounds reaching out to grab him and pull him into their hellish cursed worlds,… greedily - thirstily, and forever. He heard them speaking to him, but he couldn't understand them, their speech was garbled - muttered -

moaned, it sounded like the shriek of a witch in the dark northern woods, like the creepy croaking of frogs in the *Sumava* marshes in the south of Bohemia, like the crunching of teeth and bones of monstrous undead in a long-forgotten abandoned crematorium.

Samuel quickly packed the tools, hammers, shovels, picks, tent and food and drink into a huge forester's bag, slammed the trunk of his car and hit the road before he could think twice. He lit a cigarette and followed the directions from the sketch on the newspaper. A black cat crossed his path and meowed plaintively at Samuel. Her eyes glowed and sparkled with a greenish light - like two magical gems - crystals of chrysoberyl.

Samuel walked along the cracked road and before turning left up a gentle hill he saw a small bridge over a stream. He looked at the sketch and nodded to himself. "*This is it,*" he said to himself. He crossed the road to the other side and then crossed the bridge until he reached a dirt road. As he passed the last house down the hill, he noticed a row of apple trees that had no leaves left, but were dotted with little red apples. A sudden gust of wind shook the tree branches and Samuel instinctively stepped forward. Colourful dead leaves were falling from the surrounding deciduous trees, making a melancholic rustling sound. Samuel suddenly realized that it was almost All Saints' Day and Halloween, and that his children and his wife Laura might be browsing through the supermarket right now - on the other side of the ocean - to buy some scary costumes and pumpkins to carve.

He pictured his family's happiness, the wood burning in the fireplace, a freshly baked pumpkin pie on the table and steam rising above a huge mug of tea. He smelled cinnamon and cloves, candy, roasted meat, rotting leaves, burnt leaves in the gardens of family houses, the joyful noise of children and a swarm of masks - dead people - witches - wizards and vampires.

Samuel felt like having one of those little red apples. He walked towards one of the apple trees and didn't notice that he almost stepped on a snake - a viper - that was ready to strike. The snake could have bitten his ankle and injected a deadly venom from the glands behind its sharp fangs. But it didn't happen, Samuel moved his foot away at the last moment and the snake slithered behind a rock, where only part of its flat head and forked tongue showed. It watched Samuel with its predatory hungry eye - he was too big for it to swallow - it would have to find a vole or a squirrel.

Samuel grabbed the tempting fruit and heard the leaves in the tree tops rustle and whisper, but this time - it seemed like he heard voices and words, encoded in the wind that swayed the branches and trunks - creaking, wailing and moaning messages from the lifeless. It was as if the trees in the forest trapped forever inhuman beings, dead and horrible, vaguely hideous monsters and creatures from a parallel world - which could surely be called hell. From that grey-black dark world full of agonizing torments and shadows, sorrows and dreadful beings, here and there slyly monstrous eyes and hoarse ominous voices pierced through this bleak place. Severed hands clawed their way out from under rotting roots and headless bodies crawled from the pits dug by the fanatic mineralogists. In the sound of falling red-gold leaves, he heard the crunching of bones and the crawling of slimy creatures through the empty eye sockets of the skulls in the hill of buried corpses.

The sun suddenly broke through the cloudy sky and caressed Samuel's weary wrinkled face.

He picked an apple and bit into it eagerly, closing his eyes in anticipation of the sweet and sour treat. To his unpleasant surprise, however, the fruit tasted unusually foul and he quickly spat out the bite with a groan. He looked at where he had just bitten and saw to his horror that a monstrous wriggling worm was curling in the opening. He dropped the fruit with disgust, cursed and spat.

Samuel continued along the dirt road, but it ended at the edge of a field or rather an overgrown meadow that was fenced off with a thin wire. He remembered that the old man had mentioned this wire, he had caught something about electric current. To the right, a strip of woods ran along the side, and the wire followed it all the way up to the top of the hill.

The stranger carefully climbed over the wire and entered the private property, which he didn't care about. He walked up the hill panting as he struggled to breathe, for the slope was rather steep for his liking.

The grass was tall and dry and the sky above Samuel was dangerously low, black and grey clouds seemed heavy with leaden weights. The sun had probably hidden itself somewhere high above them for good.

He thought it was strange, he had never seen the sky hanging so low - so claustrophobically close. Somewhere from the mountain, from the ominously dark mouth of the forest, the cawing of ravens or crows echoed.

* * *

Samuel pitched a tent, grabbed a geological hammer, a magnifying glass around his neck, a block of black boards, a small black folding shovel and eagerly went to explore the mineralogical site - a quick mineralogical survey.

He found the main outcrop under a huge old oak - its exposed roots were sticking out of the dirt like the claws of a mountain beast. He saw that the hole, where the outcrop was being investigated, was partly covered. He climbed down and started digging through the mix of leaves, dark soil, and rocks. The cobwebs and mycelium were entrapping his fingers and Sam felt a disgust.

He tried to break some samples in his hand and put some in a bag that he had slung over his shoulder. He was looking for greenish *Chrysoberyl*. But that was not the only valuable stone that could be found here. There were also: blood-red *Spessartine*, blue *Beryl* and black G*ahnite*.

But Samuel had only one goal - to find a chrysoberyl crystal big enough for a jewel for a princess - big enough to cut a stone for her necklace.

Samuel suddenly cracked open one small stone and to his surprise he saw a tiny greenish translucent crystal, maybe one or two millimetres in size. He held his breath, brought the magnifying glass to his eye and positioned the stone so that it caught as much light as possible. Yes, this was chrysoberyl!

His heart raced with excitement and he felt the fever that gold miners felt on the *Klondike*. He needed to find a crystal much bigger - at least 5x5 cm - and of gem quality.

He crawled out of the pit and went for a shovel and a pickaxe. Hundreds of imaginary green crystals sparkled in his eyes and he didn't notice that a black raven was quietly watching him from the tree branches.

As Samuel was going back with the tools to the pit, he suddenly heard a kind of mad laughter of a mocking woman.

He spun around and looked towards the old overgrown clearing. It was late afternoon and Samuel felt a sudden surge of inexplicable anxiety and shivers down his spine.

He thought of Halloween in the suburbs of Chicago, America, the falling rustling gold and brown decaying leaves, the tinkling of little bells on the rafters of the old house at the end of the street - that haunted house that he always - when he was still a little boy - ran past quickly.

And again, that manic laughter came from the opposite hill in the distance. The same female voice.

And Samuel remembered the blind violinist who lived in that dreadful house, and who played by candlelight - tunes mournfully wistful, while melusines crawled through the cracks of crumbling shutters and doors.

Then he always ran quickly home to safety - he dashed past that house because he feared that the door might creak open and the violinist's bony hand would grab his arm or leg and drag him into the depths of the haunted house at the end of the street.

Samuel felt a chill of terror at the memory and the black bird in the tree tops finally made a sound: "Kraa…kraa…".

The man looked up and smiled. "I'm not alone here, after all."

He remembered his task and resumed digging. He took a small break now and then to drink water, and his gaze - every once in a while - scanned the direction of the old clearing from where he heard the woman's laughter.

He searched with his eyes among the bushes, among the old oaks and beeches, among their roots, among the boulders, among the trunks of fallen trees - to see if he could spot any ominous movement there.

Somewhere behind him, a bell jingled, a branch snapped and an owl hooted - it was getting dark slowly and Samuel felt an inexplicable grip of fear.

"Kra, kra, kra…kraaaa," cried the raven as it flew away into the distance.

"Well, now I'm left all alone with the forest monsters." he thought.

Now!

The white cloth fluttered in the dim furrow, between the trees. It looked like a forest nymph had left behind her dress, a dark and gothic garment that hid a sinister secret. Samuel leaped out of the pit, dropping his spade and leaving it buried under the roots. He hurried to the edge of the forest, where his tent was pitched on the meadow. He never thought he would be so eager to leave this place. He glanced at the sky and saw that a heavy rain had washed away the stars, leaving only a dark and ashen night. The only lights he could see were the faint glimmers from the village windows, far below. He was alone here, or so he hoped. Maybe there was someone else in the woods, someone who didn't want him here. A mad hermit, a monster, a ghost, a guardian of the gems, a killer…or a black cat with green eyes and sharp claws, the reincarnation of the cruel inquisitor Bodlig of Edelstadt. Maybe it was watching him from the branches, waiting for the right moment to pounce on him and whisper dreadful words in his ear that would make him die of fear. Samuel shook his head, trying to banish these thoughts. He didn't believe in such things, but he had read so much about them in his research that they haunted his imagination. He heard an owl hoot again, and something rustled in the grass. He jumped, startled. He smiled nervously when he saw it was just a hedgehog, but his nerves were tense as the strings of the violin that played in the house at the end of the street. The house that led to the forest path that led to the park in Schaumburg, in *Busse Woods*, on the outskirts of Chicago. The house where the tall, thin violinist lived, who was rumoured to keep corpses in his basement. Lost boys and girls who never came back, who only heard his mournful melodies at night, lullabies for the dead. Samuel had heard the neighbours whispering in the bakery, their voices scared and hushed. They said that the violinist played with those cold and stiff bodies, that he did unspeakable things to them.

The blind man never ventured out in the daylight, and his windows were draped with thick curtains that blocked out any ray of sun. The house had a weird smell, like something unspeakable was being cooked in the basement, something foul and nauseating that permeated every corner. Samuel used to pass by the house when he was a child, and he always felt a shiver down his spine. The man stood on a hill above the village, inhaling the fragrant air of the late evening. He smelled the decay of leaves, the smoke from chimneys, and his own sweat. He was no longer afraid. He had accepted his fate, whatever it was. He reached into his jacket pocket and pulled out a pack of cigarettes. His heart rate slowed down. He opened the pack and sniffed the cigarettes, a pleasant aroma. He closed his eyes in bliss. His eyelashes were oddly feminine. He took out a cigarette and put it in his mouth, thinking that the worst case scenario was that he and Laura would sell everything, move to a small and cheap apartment, and start over. As long as they were together and healthy, nothing else mattered. He nodded to himself, took out a lighter from his pants pocket and lit the cigarette. He was not worried about his family's future, he trusted that everything would be okay, he had done his best and now he knew what to do. He took a deep puff of his cigarette, holding the smoke in his lungs for a moment, then exhaling slowly. He felt a calmness wash over him, in his flesh and spirit.

Samuel Green searched and searched for many days, digging holes, exhausting himself, catching a cold and a fever. He lay in his sleeping bag in his tent, thinking that he would sell his soul to the devil if he could find the desired stone. Nothing happened, he had some hallucinations, he had a fever, he grabbed a bottle and a cigar and went outside, standing in the darkness that led him to other realms and gazing down at the valley. A bat flew by. He smoked.

He heard a voice: "Come closer to me!"

Samuel turned to the source of the dark voice. He walked towards it.

There was a man in a black hooded cloak.

The man said: "I can grant your wish…but it has a price…"

Samuel said: "Who are you?"

The man in the cloak said: "Nathrengar - Lord of Darkness. You can call me Nat, for short."

Samuel said: "And why should I trust you? If you're the Dark Lord, then I'm Snow White."

Nat said: "So…you don't want to find the stone? The chrysoberyl…"

Samuel said: "How the heck,…how do you know?"

Samuel added hastily: "What do you want from me for that stone?"

Nat said: "Just a small thing, my friend, just sign your name - in the Book of Darkness."

Samuel said: "And when I die…you will come for me…like in the fairy-tales?"

Nat laughed his eerie and piercing laugh, making Samuel dizzy with the sudden sound.

He said: "No, I'm busy, pal, it will probably be someone else who will take you…someone you won't expect at all,…that's how it usually goes,…I'm here by chance, Samuel,…when your time comes,…I'll probably be spreading darkness with my Dungwu's army in another galaxy or a parallel universe,…who knows,…I have a lot to do!"

Samuel was baffled, he never thought that someone like the devil could be so friendly or casual with a human. He wondered if hell was not as bad as he imagined.

Samuel said: "Okay,…and how many years will you give me, Nat?"

Nat responded: "I will let you live as long as you were meant to live - the full span that was given to your body…"

Samuel said: "And can I ask, how much that would be? How much would have I left?"

Nat would have laughed heartily if he had a heart, but instead of a heart, he had something so horrible, something so repulsive, that you wouldn't want to know what it was. But he laughed anyway, with the laugh of a hungry monster. A monster that craved blood and soul, and needed a constant supply of both. And the more he got, the more he wanted - to satisfy his thirst. There was no room for mercy - where the heart should be, there was a black box, and in that box...

Nat said: "So do you want the stone or not? Make up your mind now, I don't have time for nonsense. We either make a deal or we don't."

Nathrengar took out a golden pyramid from his pocket. The monolith was decorated with red crystals. He watched Samuel with a grin and toyed with the shiny object.

Samuel looked at the mysterious stranger and then burst into laughter. "Man, you almost got me, what kind of scam are you running? Go to hell! Get lost!"

Samuel turned his back to the weird figure and walked back to his tent without looking back.

"You know,...I was going to give you a dream,...you would fly up through the chimney like everyone else, sooner or later anyway,...and you didn't even made use of your life wisely,...Laura would be happy,...happy with you,...but whatever,..." the stranger's voice sighed from behind Sam, from the dark depths of the forest. This was way too tempting notion for the man to resist.

Samuel stopped for a moment in front of his tent and listened to the silence that suddenly fell over the woods. Then he unzipped the tent and gasped!

The dark lord was sitting inside the tent!

Nathrengar was there, playing with the pyramid.

Samuel's heart pounded like a machine.

He could only see the Dark Lord's shape now - his sharp teeth clicking horribly and his eyeless white form. Or maybe he had eyes, but they were so black and sunken in his skull that they were invisible. Nathrengar smiled in a friendly way, but when he parted his bloody rotten lips, he said: "Are you sure you do not want to think it through?"

Samuel felt dizzy again and had to cover his mouth and nose because of the terrible smell that made him nauseous. Nathrengar leapt up, flew through the air towards Samuel and grabbed him by the neck with a menacing grip. Then he sniffed him and licked him hungrily, letting a monstrous tongue slide down his neck and baring his fangs as if he wanted to bite and suck his blood like a werewolf. But then he changed his mind and pushed him away in disgust. "Phew! You have so much pure light in you, you sicken me, Sam! What kind of freak are you, not giving in slowly?"

"Then give up! I'm offering you one last chance. Do you want to live or die?"

"Think of Laura, your kids, you'll have a good life,...I'll tell you how,...What if you die tomorrow? Who will take care of them?"

"So what?"

Tears stream down Samuel's face spontaneously, like a little boy. He shakes his head.

"Yes,..." he whispered softly.

Nathrengar grinned and turned his dragon head. "What? Did I hear right? You said yes?"

"Yes!" Samuel said firmly.

Nathrengar approached Samuel - his prey - and pulled out a black book from under his long black cloak. He tapped it with a scary hand. "This is the Book of Darkness, and you will sign it now!"

The Lord of Darkness flipped through the book impatiently until black flies flew out of it and crawled over his face: "Hmm,…here,…you sign for me, my dear Samuel…"

Samuel leaned over the book with fear but curiosity and looked for some pen.

Nathrengar laughed and cackled maliciously and pulled out a dagger. "Here! Please, sir," he says mockingly and fences with the knife blade that sparks with hellfire in the light of the cold dead moon. "Sign with your blood, mate! You know the drill,…"

Samuel stood there indecisively.

"Then you cut yourself or should I do it?…With my claw,…it's sharp…"

"Here, take it…" he hands him the dagger.

Samuel grabbed the knife and cut himself slightly, so there was not much blood.

"You're making a fool out of me,…but you're a brave one,…I'll give you that,…put it here…" Nathrengar snatched it from his hand.

Then he came closer and smiled, took his hand and with a great pleasure and very slowly he made a deep cut in his palm. Samuel screamed and writhed in pain.

Then he took Samuel's other hand by the index finger and dipped it in the pool of blood in the palm of his hand.

"It's a nice signature, my friend."

"So,… that's it…"

Samuel raised his head. "So, what happens next?"

"You go to sleep now and tomorrow you will find the stone! It was a pleasure doing business with you, Samuel."

Samuel looked up from his signature in the Book of Darkness. "And how did you appear here, by chance?"

Nathrengar laughed: "You know that idiom - *think of the devil and there he appears…*", he closed the book producing a loud clapping noise. He tapped it with his monstrous sharp claw.

"Don't forget - you'll find that stone tomorrow. Enjoy it with Laura,…well,…I have to go,…it was nice to meet you, Sam,…indeed you were a good man…"

Nathrengar spat with a disgust on the ground until fire and smoke appeared.

Then he chuckled: "Good and pure, but this will surely change…!"

"Greed will lead you to a dark fate - don't forget - everyone can feel jealousy and see your wealth that you can't conceal from them."

Nathrengar pulled out a golden pyramid and pushed one of the crystals in so a beam shot for the stars.

The Lord of Darkness turned into a spark that flew in the direction along that beam.

Only smoke and smell of hell remained in the air long after the Dark Lord vanished.

"And, I thought it was the other way around, that the devil lives underground…" Samuel contemplated.

"You can't hide big money, Sam,…" a dark voice echoed from the ominously twinkling stars.

Samuel turned towards the dark entrance which hid the pegmatite outcrops with precious stones.

The zigzag roots of massive trees were like the limbs of monster.

Samuel could feel a burning touch of the Nathrengar's dark green evil eyes,…patiently waiting for his unfortunate soul.

Every treasure has its price!

To Be Continued

King & Bard

Once upon a time, there was a king who was very lonely. He had no friends, and he didn't know how to have fun. There are many reasons why the king might have been lonely. He might have been too busy with his royal duties to have time for friends. He might have been afraid to trust people, because he was worried that they would betray him. Or he might have simply not met anyone who he felt a connection with.

One day, the king was walking through the kingdom when he heard a beautiful song coming from a nearby village. He followed the sound and found the Bard singing in a field. The king was so impressed by the Bard's talent that he invited him to come to the castle and be his court bard.

The Bard was honoured to accept the king's invitation, and he soon became one of the king's most trusted advisors. He used his songs and stories to teach the king about the world and to help him make wise decisions. The king was grateful for the Bard's friendship and guidance, and he knew that he was lucky to have him in his life.

The bard arrived at the castle and told the king a story about a brave knight who saved a princess from a dragon. The king was so impressed by the story that he asked the bard to stay at the castle and tell him more stories.

The bard agreed, and he and the king became friends. The king would often ask the bard to tell him stories, and the bard would always oblige. The king learned a lot from the bard, and he became a much happier person.

Here is one of the stories that the Bard told the King about the Arab world and Islam:

Once upon a time, there was a young man named Ali who lived in a small village in the Arab world. Ali was a kind and generous person, but he was also very poor. One day, Ali was walking through the village when he saw a group of people gathered around a man who was giving a speech. The man was talking about Islam, and he was saying that Islam was the true religion and that it would bring peace and prosperity to the world. Ali was intrigued by what the man was saying, and he decided to learn more about Islam.

Ali began to study the Quran and the teachings of the Prophet Muhammad. He also began to pray and fast. As he learned more about Islam, Ali became more and more convinced that it was the true religion. He also became more and more determined to live his life according to the teachings of Islam.

One day, Ali was walking through the village when he saw a group of people who were being harassed by a group of bullies. Ali knew that he had to help, so he stepped in and stood up to the bullies. The bullies were surprised by Ali's courage, and they backed down. The people who had been harassed were grateful to Ali for his help, and they told him that he was a hero.

Ali was happy to have helped, and he was proud to be a Muslim. He knew that Islam was the true religion, and he was determined to live his life according to its teachings.

The moral of the story is that Islam is a religion of peace and love, and that it can bring peace and prosperity to the world. It is also a religion of courage and justice, and it teaches us to stand up for what is right.

One day, the king came to the bard with a request. He asked the bard to write a story about him. The bard agreed, and he spent the next few weeks writing a story about the king. When the story was finished, the king was very pleased. He read the story to his advisors, and they all agreed that it was a very good story. The king was so happy that he decided to give the bard a gift.

The king gave the bard a golden lute. The lute was very beautiful, and the bard was very happy to receive it. He promised the king that he would use the lute to write more stories.

And the Bard wrote this story:

Once upon a time, there was an immortal soul who travelled from universe to universe. The soul was always on the run, being chased by a black hole agent. The agent was determined to capture the soul and take it to the black hole, where it would be destroyed. The soul was always one step ahead of the agent, but it was starting to get tired. The agent was getting closer and closer, and the soul knew that it couldn't outrun it forever. One day, the soul was running through a universe when it saw a planet. The planet was beautiful, and the soul felt a sense of peace that it hadn't felt in a long time. The soul decided to land on the planet and take a break. The soul was resting on the planet when it saw a human. The human was beautiful, and the soul felt a sense of love that it hadn't felt in a long time. The soul knew that it had found its home. The agent was still chasing the soul, but the soul no longer cared. The soul had found love, and that was all that mattered. The agent eventually caught up to the soul, but the soul didn't fight back. The agent took the soul to the black hole, but the soul was no longer afraid. The soul knew that it would be with its love forever. The agent was surprised by the soul's reaction, had never seen anything like it before. The agent thought that the soul would be scared, but the soul was calm and peaceful and the agent didn't know what to do. The agent had never been in this situation before. He didn't know if the soul was real or not, but he knew that the soul was special. The agent decided to let the soul go, he didn't know why, but the he felt like it was the right thing to do. The soul was released, and it flew back to its love. The soul was happy to be reunited with its love, and knew that it would never be alone again.

The agent watched as the soul flew away and didn't know what to think. He had never been so conflicted before and didn't know if he had made the right decision, but knew that would never forget the soul.

The king was very pleased with this story and started pondering about where he could find love like that soul in the story.

The bard and the king continued to be friends for many years. The bard would often come to the castle to tell the king stories, and the king would always listen. The king was always happy to hear the bard's stories, and he learned a lot from them.

However, nothing lasts forever, except for *Jannah* - the Allah's eternal kingdom paradise, and the Bard had disappeared and never ever came to see the king again.

The king was so sad!

He didn't eat and didn't drink and became ill.

He was strolling his kingdom for ages.

One day the king arrived to some ancient gate in the middle of old impenetrable forest and entered different world, for he never knew it was a portal to get to the parallel universe.

In one beautiful city with white houses and gardens he met a beautiful princess.

He was unable to stop thinking about her.

But in that world he was not a king, he was nobody…

He even didn't understand the language.

Nevertheless, he found something new,…so precious, and he felt he was born again…

Now, when he lost everything, he found everything,…for a pure love entered his heart - one more time.

And he decided, that he will become somebody - not by the inheritance, but by his own will and effort!

STORY 8

The Gem for Princess

The wind whistles and moans in the empty shaft of this hotel, caressing Samuel's ears with its haunting melody. He relishes the feeling, letting it seep into his soul. He's trapped in this place, but He doesn't mind. Time is an illusion, and He'll succeed sooner or later.

He's serene and composed.

He's bold and brave.

Because tonight, He had witnessed them - The Illuminators, who came to him in his dream.

They revealed to him that he was dreaming - right now,…right then…

The first one was a man who radiated like a golden star.

He was clad like a secret agent, with a briefcase and a tailored suit.

He looked like he belonged to a bygone era, scanning the windows of the house in the night.

The street lamp illuminated his towering shadow on the wall, making him look like a silent film hero.

Samuel was so captivated by his aura, he turned around to look for the camera and crew.

But all he found behind him was garbage and bins.

***

Sam turned his gaze back to the being - the man - who was surrounded by a yellow halo of light.

He was looking at Sam. He was silent, but he was speaking to him - transmitting to him some kind of message or wisdom.

Samuel felt love, kindness, compassion and encouragement!

And then it dawned on him like a revelation!

This is just a dream, He's lying in bed in his hotel room and this is just a dream.

But it was the most vivid dream ever, it felt more real than life.

And then Samuel received the message for the second time!

THIS IS THE TRUE REALITY!

The emissary of light was shining at Sam and was imparting to him the wisdom of the shamans.

THIS IS THE REAL YOU!

REMEMBER THIS WHEN YOU WAKE UP!

SHARE IT WITH EVERYONE!

FROM NOW ON WE'LL COME TO VISIT YOU, EVERY NOW AND THEN...

***

He was amazed and scanned the area to see two more glowing figures, one very tall and one short and plump.

All of them were dressed in suits, all three of them radiated warm yellow.

The chubby man came closer to Samuel, reducing the distance.

He thought to himself, *well, it looks so real, but now He knows this is just a dream when He sleeps.*

But the godfather-like character gestured to somewhere behind Samuel and He turned that way.

Suddenly Sam found himself in some kind of spa, it was not a sauna, but rather a different kind of wellness facility.

It was still night and it felt like an ancient Roman bathhouse…

This is where the notes end and the rest of the story I have reconstructed from my research on Mr. Samuel Green. I have visited many libraries, I have traced his steps from his journey and talked with the people Samuel had encountered on his trip to Europe. It seemed to me that Samuel Green had undergone some kind of awakening and I felt I had to share his story in full.

* * *

Samuel landed at an ancient, forgotten, archaeological site by the sea.

They were the ruins of a spa from the Roman Empire.

But what was odd was that people were bathing there, they were completely nude.

"Touch them!" ordered a voice behind him.

Sam spun to see the plump guy in the suit. He wore a snow-white suit and a red rose in his buttonhole, a moustache over his mouth and a big grin.

Above their heads the sun was blazing as it slid across the azure sky, and the splashing of the waves of the serene emerald sea filled their ears.

"Hey, it's you,…" Sam mumbled.

"But I don't know you at all," he added inquisitively.

"You wouldn't comprehend this, but you can call me Alex," answered the chubby man.

"But you have a belly!" Sam remarked, then cringed at his unintended, unexpected candour and wanted to apologize right away, smooth it over somehow.

But the man in the white suit - and now Sam noticed also the white hat - just smiled and then laughed heartily "That's a three-pear-belly, son."

"What?" wondered Samuel.

"Well, I just, uh, I just like to eat well, donuts, grilled chicken, XXL cappuccino and stuff,…haha."

"Yeah, and myself too," answered Sam.

Walking by Samuel was a gorgeous girl with long black hair that had such a stunning metallic indigo shine.

Samuel turned and gaped at her in astonishment because she stopped right next to him and because she was totally nude.

The girl was looking straight at Sam, or more precisely - through him - as if she didn't notice the man at all.

She had such a weird look in her eyes, so dreamy, she was smiling faintly, but in those eyes,…in those eyes - there was a sorrow and also love, a lot of love.

Alex smiled knowingly and shook his head.

Suddenly, the wind rose and thunder growled in the distance - ever so softly - as if the storm was testing what it could get away with.

"Come on, touch her, Samuel!"

Samuel tentatively reached out and touched the girl's shoulder and the shoulder was pleasantly warm and the skin velvety smooth - lightly sprinkled with sea water.

Samuel took a deep breath, as if he had finally started to really breathe, and his ears caught the sound of the waves caressing gently the sea shore, the pebbles and the cliffs. Somewhere above his head, a seagull cried, but only softly, as if to welcome him from above.

And again!

Samuel took another breath and saw the mysterious man in the white hat approaching with a smile.

Sam was puzzled because the beautiful, bronzed girl didn't pay him any attention at all - apparently she didn't sense Sam's touch at all.

It was like that, she was unaware of him.

And Samuel was shocked.

"Am I dead? I am a ghost,… right Alex?"

And he turned towards the plump man.

"But you, Alex, see me, hear me,…and I see you,…so are You also a ghost?"

"Where are we?"

"Alex!"

Alex chuckled, then roared like a beast, and shook his head resolutely.

"It's a bit more complicated."

Samuel now tried to touch Alex, but his hand just went through the well-dressed fellow without any resistance.

"Dude, it's like in that show - *Quantum Leap,...*" Samuel said in disbelief.

"You're missing the point, tiger," Alex replied.

Sam noticed a large palm tree behind the guy and watched its leaves sway in the wind.

He could clearly hear the noises they made and the sun that slipped through them, here and there, dazzling him with its brilliance.

The splash of ripples reached his ears and delightfully touched the auditory system within, which sent signals back through the neural network to the brain that told him - *this is very nice and you feel great.*

The little frogs in the nearby pond behind tall grass were ominously laughing.

"So what's the deal then?" Sam folded his arms angrily.

"Are we in a computer game?"

"I can feel everything, touch, hear the waves - the sea - leaves fluttering in the wind - I can smell that girl - her skin - cigarettes from you - Alex!"

"When did you last brush your teeth?"

Alex laughed, but casually and somewhat sheepishly rubbed his index finger over his teeth.

"Your candour impresses me, Sam, I just hope that out there in "LIFE" on Earth, you're that bold too!"

Meanwhile, the girl was walking away and dipping her body in the outdoor bath - a small pool in the rock.

There were other people in it.

All nude.

Both men watched her with rapt attention.

Alex whispered into Samuel's ear "She's a beauty huh?"

Samuel nodded his head.

Alex added "Well, it's like this, you're just sleeping now and all this seems to you, well, and at the same time it doesn't seem,…it's just another reality - another universe - working on a different frequency - and having divergent rules - laws of physics, if you will…"

Samuel watched the girl and admired her curves and dreamily muttered "Beautiful rules."

The plump man whispered mysteriously into Samuel's ear: "Your body on Earth is sleeping and recharging energy - but at the same time you are here - in another one of your bodies, and at the same time you exist infinitely many times in infinitely many bodies in infinitely many universes and experience infinitely many adventures in space and time with no end and no beginning,… isn't that amazing?"

***

The waves surged over each other like racing horses, and now and then there was the faint cry of seagulls.

Samuel turned to ask the guy something, but he vanished - dissolved - only a tall white Roman marble statue stood there.

All around were palm trees and the relics of ancient Roman baths.

Above them in the distance spread vast sand dunes.

It was curious that the statue and the columns around it had endured the ravages of time, while the buildings made of concrete and red bricks had collapsed to the point where mostly foundations or low cracked walls remained.

Once this was the place of Roman Baths and just a moment ago Samuel was in that time back 100 years BC!

But now it's all gone - swept away by the sand from the hourglass.

As if he had traveled back and forth in time.

Samuel wandered through the ruins, listening to the roar of the ocean and the flutter of palm leaves overhead.

In the distance below, the surface of the water sparkled emerald in colour and was rippled by kite surfers and boats.

The man was exploring the archaeological site with curiosity.

Oh - here was once the *Apodyterium* - changing room - and there - *Palaestrae* - something like today's gym - and a little further - *Natatio* - open swimming pool.

A little while ago, the beautiful Goddess was dipping her enchanting bronzed body into it.

Where did she go? What was her story?

Samuel walked on, looking at the - *Calidarium* - the sauna, heated by the hot water of the pool, and after a few steps he came to the - *Frigidarium* - the cooling pool - the heart of the Roman Baths,

a Dome of colossal dimensions once stood here.

Suddenly - as if by magic - the walls soared into the sky, which was covered by a ceiling lavishly decorated with frescoes.

The pool filled with water and naked figures materialized from the cold air - they passed by Samuel without noticing him - Samuel was touching them and felt the touch, their skin was tepid and damp.

The spa guests walking the colonnade past Sam didn't even glance.

The man had a panic attack - he was a ghost after all!

He suddenly felt so alone and it was a terrifying state of mind!

He started trembling all over, his legs went limp and he couldn't breathe.

As if some evil force was crushing his lungs.

Monster.

Out of nowhere, a figure in a black cloak and a black hat emerged from the ceiling.

And he spoke in a raspy voice "Sam,…Sam!"

"Who are you? What are you?"

Samuel noticed that the mysterious being had a Salvador Dalí moustache and welding goggles.

A creature in a long black cloak descended the vertical brick walls of the Pantheon until it stood directly in front of Samuel.

In his hand - or rather in his raven claw - he held a newspaper and in his other hand he held a wand.

He handed the newspaper to a stunned Samuel.

He looked at it - they were obviously very old, yellowed and almost crumbling in his shaking hands.

He could smell their musty odour.

The newspaper was written in Spanish.

He was looking at a photograph of some famous artist.

Under the picture was written: "*Salvador Felip Jacint Dalí i Doménech, Agosto 1931, La Persistencia de la Memoria - The Persistence of Memory*".

Then, the gaze of Samuel shifted a bit upwards, there was a headline printed in large thick orange letters "S*oy Genio - I'm Genius." and below that was another smaller headline: "Recuérdame Simpre De Esta Manera! - Always Remember Me This Way!*"

"But, why,…" Samuel muttered a little relieved that someone was talking to him, that he could hear a human voice.

The man in the black hat rasped "Follow me, Monsieur, suis-moi s'il te plait!"

"But,…" Samuel exclaimed in confusion.

But already the weirdo in welding goggles was running up the spiral stairs that suddenly descended from the ceiling, helping himself with a cane that he had frantically tapped the stone floor.

"Dépêche-toi Samuel!"

Samuel felt a surge of panic as he saw the mysterious stranger vanish up the spiral staircase. He couldn't bear the thought of being left behind in this haunted place, like a ghost trapped in limbo.

He sprinted after him, hoping to catch a glimpse of his dark cloak or hear the tap of his wand.

The staircase seemed to have no end, twisting and turning into the gloom.

Along the way, he encountered bizarre creatures that were slithering, crawling, and hopping down from above. Samuel recoiled at the sight of their hideous faces and deformed limbs. He feared they would shove him down into the bottomless pit below.

But his fear of loneliness was stronger than his fear of falling, so he kept climbing up the infinite spiral. His breath was ragged, his heart was hammering, his chest was burning. He wondered how long he could endure this ordeal.

Then he heard it: music. It was a music box that played a cheerful tune, as if to mock his misery. He quickened his pace.

The stranger's voice echoed in his ears, taunting him with a maniacal laugh.

"Uno - dos - tres - uno - dos - tres,…hurry up, Samuel!" The voice belonged to a lunatic in welding glasses, who had lured Samuel into this tower that pierced the dark clouds of Mordor.

The music from the antique jukebox grew louder as Samuel reached the summit of the stairs.

"Uno - dos - tres - uno - dos - tres,… don't give up, Samuel, don't give up…uno - dos - tres - uno - dos - tres…"

Samuel stumbled towards the heavy door that stood between him and the stranger. But it was locked. He heard the lunatic's voice from inside, cursing and laughing.

"Where are you, man, merde?!" he bellowed from behind the door.

"I don't have a key, the door is locked, dammit!" Samuel gasped, clutching his chest.

He collapsed to the ground, his hand reaching for the iron doorknob.

Then everything went black.

***

Samuel opened his eyes and found himself in a room with a man in black hovering over him. The man was giving him first aid, pressing on his chest rhythmically. "Uno - dos - tres - quatro - uno - dos - tres - quatro…" he muttered in a raspy voice as he performed CPR (*cardiopulmonary resuscitation*).

Then he leaned in closer to Samuel and puckered his lips, ready to give him mouth-to-mouth resuscitation. He looked like a psychopath in his black tight sweatpants and long black coat, as if he wanted to kiss Samuel instead of saving him. Samuel felt a wave of nausea as he smelled the oniony breath and the stickiness emanating from the man. He noticed that he was wearing a mask of Salvador Dalí - a cheap mask from some Chinese store, a mask for three Euros, a mask for Halloween.

"Get the fuck out!" Samuel screamed in terror.

But the man was not deterred and ripped off his mask to reveal another face - or rather, another disguise. He tossed his broadsword into the corner with a loud clang and let his black wig fall to the floor. A small rat peeked out from behind his hood, where he had hidden a pair of thick glasses.

The old man's lips, painted with red lipstick in a sloppy manner, approached Samuel's mouth again. Samuel felt a surge of disgust as he saw the powdered cheeks and smelled the awful combination of onion and cheap cologne.

"Haha,…you're such an ungrateful rascal,…I saved your life,…and you yell at me like that?" the old man said in a mocking tone.

"Fuck off, dude, get away from me!" Samuel shouted and pushed the old man hard, making him stumble.

* * *

"Would you like some wine?" asked another man who was sitting behind a desk.

Samuel snapped out of his horrible nightmare and sat up. "Where…? Who are you?" he asked the man in the black hat and wig.

He walked to a large oak table and collapsed into a massive chair covered with furs.

"Please, allow me to introduce myself. Baron,…um,…Vaudeville - that's my name." The stranger bowed. He had the same Salvador Dali moustache as before, but this time it was real. He was holding a wand in his hand. He poured red wine into two medieval goblets and slid one in front of Samuel. He lifted his goblet in a toast and said: "So, how about a toast to - to - um,…maybe to the princess?"

Samuel barely dipped his lips in the wine, keeping an eye on the baron. He didn't trust him at all. He had no idea what he was up to.

"So, what do you think, Sir? American,...how do you like it?" Salvador Dali alias Baron Vaudeville asked eagerly.

"Hey, this is damn good, this wine, what is it?" Samuel asked, taking a sip.

"Tempranillo, mon ami, vintage 1789," Baron Vaudeville said casually.

"Shit! You're kidding..."

"Non, non, mon ami, how does it taste? This wine,...describe it to me!"

"Hmm, uh, it's so spicy - harsh and,..." Samuel struggled to find words.

Baron Vaudeville leaned forward with anticipation and parted his lips slightly, ready to pounce like a hungry vampire.

"I don't know, but I feel - some kind of power - but that power is ...".

"Well?" Baron Vaudeville whispered, playing nervously with his wand.

Samuel noticed that the wand had a head of Satan with eyes like two precisely cut rubies and horns of ivory.

"Violence, some kind of incredible will,..." Samuel said, covering his mouth instinctively.

"Bingo!" the baron exclaimed.

"Music!" he shouted towards the ornate baroque chandelier which shook violently and crashed on the table.

Samuel felt a sudden dizziness and saw everything around him in a blur. The room transformed into a hall where Spanish and

Moroccan musicians from Andalusia played and where many guests danced and stomped and clapped. Everything was happening in a wild rhythm. Samuel stood bewildered in the middle and the ecstatic crowd danced around him.

The world spun around Samuel. Suddenly, Baron Vaudeville emerged from the dancing crowd. He was wearing brocade pants and shoes made of sparkling diamonds. A red turban on his head - like a maharaja - and a wand in his hand. He danced towards Samuel and started hitting him on the head with the wand.

"Why? What are you,…" Sam yelled. "Stop it, you idiot!"

But the baron ignored his words and hit him and hit him until he bled, and the crowd cheered and laughed and joined in. They hit him with chairs, fists, stabbed with forks and chicken bones. They spat on him and trampled on him. Samuel sobbed. He was in pain. This was an ending that he had never imagined in the darkest moments of his life.

Baron Vaudeville leaned over and whispered in his ear, "That wine has power - it's from the year the Bastille fell - only by force can something be changed, Samuel - only by force, mon ami."

***

Then Samuel remembered his wife and children, and woke up.

He pulled out a picture of them and cried until he shivered. *"I'm sorry, I'm so sorry for everything…"* *"Where are you, where are you?"* he whispered and sobbed.

"If I could,…what could I,…nothing could I…all is lost in the past,…" the homeless man moaned, crawling out of his sleeping bag and startling another rat that ran from under the dumpster.

Suddenly he heard music, an Arabic tune, and turned just as a car entered the street, shining with all colours. The car had transparent walls and flashed blue and red and orange and green and yellow. It was a Ferrari, but one he had never seen in his life - it was like something from the future. The door swung upward like a butterfly flapping its wings.

The driver leaned towards him and shouted "Get in!"

As if in a trance, Samuel stumbled and climbed timidly inside - he sank into a comfortable seat. The man was wearing a bright orange Arabic robe, a cap with the inscription and logo "FC Barcelona" and a bright confident smile. "Would you like some tea, Samuel?" the man asked him.

"Yes." Samuel said, shivering from the cold.

The man smiled, produced a tray with glasses and a kettle from somewhere that was steaming. "This is Atai bil Na'na' - or Moroccan green tea with mint - it will warm you up and get you on your feet, Sam."

"How do you know my name sir?"

A man in an orange robe poured a green hot liquid into a small glass with Arabic ornaments and with a smile answered "The ways of Allah are mysterious…"

And with those words and a smile, he handed the glass to the shivering homeless man. Then he poured one for himself and looked up and whispered "*Hamdulillah*".

Samuel took a sip and looked gratefully at the benefactor. "And how come I don't know you, sir?"

"I'm,…haha,…people in the neighbourhood call me - Mr. Melange."

"Hmm, interesting name - and why do they call you that?"

"Well, I don't know, maybe because I like to mix things - blend them together,…" Mr. Melange smiled.

It was then that Samuel noticed that the man's robes were indeed glowing - emitting an orange phosphorescent light.

"I,… I think I know - You are an angel - my guardian angel." Samuel whispered in awe with a sudden insight.

Mr. Melange laughed heartily and loudly, "Well, it's all a bit more complicated, I'd rather call myself Neighbourhood Watch," and with these words he put on white gloves.

"Then let's put on some cheerful music and go for a ride, shall we?!" he said, looking into Samuel's eyes.

With these words he touched the control panel and wondered aloud what to choose for the music.

"Something cheerful, I guess." "Do you like Chinese disco, Sam?"

"And where are we going?" Samuel asked, tears shining in his eyes.

Mr. Melange noticed this and looked away as if he didn't see anything. He thought for a moment and then smiled. "Look, I know very well what you've been through Samuel, you've had a hard life, many wounds and humiliations. But I can - on behalf of our team - tell you, that you did great - and I can say, that for your performance - or rather,…your life - you deserve 5 stars out of five - I'll give you only the best review and the highest rating."

Samuel smiled in confusion but said: "Thank you Mr. Melange, you made my day, thank you very much."

"Even though I may be starting to understand, I still feel lost,…" he added, looking at the driver.

Music started to play from the walls of the car.

"This is only a dream, Samuel, but one day you will wake up and see and understand…"

"So where are we going?"

"Well, to eat, to put something warm in our stomachs, to Chinatown to the *Seven Treasures* - they make great curry and Hong Kong style iced tea, or hot coffee if you prefer." and with these words he reversed wildly out of the back alley, and then they sped through the streets of Chicago towards Wentworth Avenue.

The car zooms towards Downtown on South Wacker Drive, passing by the Willis Tower with its two enormously tall antennas sticking out into the red sky like two devil's horns. It's no coincidence that the skyscraper's zip code is 60606. This is the Lincoln's City and Al Capone's City. A windy city that constantly changes its face. Sometimes it is demonic and cruel, sometimes it is friendly. You never know what awaits you around the next corner. The karmic wheel spins at a dizzying speed here.

You can find Samuel after midnight in the restaurant Seven Treasures as he sips Jasmine tea, which is free here. Then he would have to endure another freezing morning in the park - five hours - before they open the Tasty Place cafe. To keep warm and survive the harsh five hours outside - he usually exercises in the park - in the children's playground with swings and a carousel. Seven Treasures closes at two in the morning and Tasty Place opens before seven. So, you can also talk to him there and buy him a hot coffee for a dollar. He will appreciate it. Sometimes he basks on the steps of the West Alexander Street church and eats cheap apples from a vendor friend who sometimes even gives him something for free.

But wait, this is not the end, rather the beginning.

There are ups and downs in life and the change is the only assurance.

Who is Samuel Green and what does he have to say to us?

Let's listen to the rest of his story!

The man opened his eyes - to find that he was lying in a sleeping bag - in a tent…

When Samuel woke up in the morning, he realized that it was all just a dream and a nightmare, in which his fervent wish was reflected - to find a large Chrysoberyl crystal. The kind that could be cut and set into a princess necklace. A gem big enough to earn him the fortune he desired. Samuel heated soy milk on the portable stove and ate his favourite donut with apricot jam. He then took out a pack of cigarettes in a steel case and a yellow plastic lighter. He hesitated for a long time whether to smoke or not. He was thinking… He was thinking that next time he should buy a bigger car - a four-wheel drive, or at least an SUV, so that he could carry heavier tools with him or even hire some diggers. That is, if he ever wanted to come back here again. But after several days of exhausting digging, he was quite skeptical. However, something crossed his mind as he pondered and the woodpecker tapped loudly on the bark of a tree, somewhere in the branches above his head. He grimaced, put a cigarette in the corner of his mouth and lit it with gusto.

The woodpecker kept tapping the tree to find his breakfast too - just like Samuel. Samuel smiled at the idea of everyone always looking for something. Life is a frantic treasure hunt. He reached out into the grass and blew smoke in a pattern, watching the swaying trees and listening to the soft wind as it rustled through the glistening leaves.

Samuel casually grabbed the muffler and pulled out some kind of corded sticks. He grinned. He placed the dynamite on his chest and put his hands under his head and imagined blowing up everything here. He bought the explosive from gypsies in Ostrava - they could find and sell anything, anything! Well, he couldn't use it yet, he didn't want to cause a stir in the nearby village and have the police on his tail. But today, a strong storm was forecasted - so he could theoretically time the explosion after a loud thunder. However, he would have to calculate very well, but that would come later - God willing. Later, Samuel crawled into the tent to get some rest for the night's action. He curled up in his sleeping bag and tried to sleep. Just take a nap. And he did.

As Samuel was lying in the sleeping bag, he suddenly heard the sound of a zipper being slowly opened and a low, wailing groan. Something like a castrated dog barking in the distance and the echoes reaching Sam's ears through the morning mist. He also heard birds singing, so it must still be morning. He had a strange thought that crossed his mind now, a strange but persistent thought - he always thought he had a devilish name - SAMUEL… He came from a Jewish family, and the name was quite common there, but still, he had a peculiar aversion to churches and faith since he was young, and he was more interested in black magic and liked to walk alone in the woods at night. He often felt his head, trying to sense something in his skull. But now he laughed because he thought of horns - devilish horns. "*You really are a fool, Sam!*" he muttered to himself. Then, however, his eyes fell on the zipper of the tent, which was being opened slowly and carefully. Now it was serious! Samuel drew a hunting knife from the sheath at his belt with lightning speed - like a true backwoodsman. Deer horn handle and "Stainless Steel" blade. He sat up and was ready to defend himself and kill - if necessary.

He had trained in Krav-maga in his youth and was pretty good with and without a knife, so he was ready for asymmetrical combat, for a real encounter with anyone or anything. But life can surprise you with hellish twists.

Nothing happened for a while, there was silence. Then he heard a soft squeak and then a snort. Then a fox stuck its head into the tent and looked at Samuel curiously.

RABIES!

That was the very first thing that popped into his mind. And he remembered the numerous signs on tree trunks, warning about foxes and other animals…

"Get the fuck out!" Sam swore in surprise in his native language.

But the fox just yawned to show its sharp teeth and long thin tongue.

So this is different… A little scratch is all it takes here… And it's rabid! Unless he had a gun or another firearm, which he didn't. The fox moved closer to Sam who froze. It wasn't that obvious at first glance, but the man realized with horror that the bold and mad animal was crawling towards him - slowly but surely. Sam glanced at the knife blade out of the corner of his eye, then quickly back at the fox. He wondered how to deal with this dangerous situation. But then he was horrified by another thought - how did the fox unzip the tent?!

He didn't know - at that moment - what he would find out later…

***

As the rain started to fall softly outside, it would have been soothing to hear its gentle tapping on the tent's tarpaulin, but not today. Today it sounded more like a drumbeat in a circus, announcing some daring escapade. Sam felt a flash of memory from his childhood. He used to live in Chinatown in Chicago, where there was a mural painted on a brick wall near his house. It was a colourful and artistic work by Rich Lo, who signed his name at the bottom corner above the sidewalk. The mural depicted four characters: the Monkey King, a Chinese princess, a trapeze artist and an ancient Chinese warrior in armour. Sam always stopped and admired the painting whenever he passed by. He felt a strange attraction to the mural, as if it had some magic power over him. He especially liked the princess, who was the largest and most central figure. She was making some kind of hand gesture with her fingers, which Sam suspected had a spiritual meaning. And her eyes - slanted beautifully along her nose - seemed to lock him in place, as if he couldn't move. He felt completely absorbed by her mesmerising gaze - and now he realised he had been hypnotised. He didn't have to go far - he just had to stay still and focus entirely on one thing. It was a form of meditation, the ultimate concentration on one thing at one moment. Samuel learned throughout his life that things should be done well or not at all. Unfortunately, in today's world, there are so many distractions that people lose this ability. Instead, they develop many ailments and addictions, such as mobile phones, overeating, coffee, cigarettes, television, drugs, sugar and salt, money and work, what others think, someone specific, porn, sex, life achievements. There are many traps that we can fall into and go round and round. And the circle leads nowhere - it's a bewitched path.

People are so restless, aimless and agitated, as if they were possessed by demons! Their minds are erratic - they are like carrier pigeons - you wave your flags to the left and they move in that direction and so on. We humans think that we are different from animals, but it is not entirely true - our minds are - for the majority of individuals - collective. You just have to look at Wenceslas Square in Czech Republic the other day to see how the people are holding red cards and chanting that they no longer want this puppet president, but that they want another one. Who gave them the cards? Who pulled them out of the comfort of their armchairs in the living room? From the hockey match to stay in the league. The Billboards, pictograms, TV news…

Illuminati, freemasons, oligarchs, puppeteers, people so rich that it would be inappropriate to list them in the ranking of Forbes magazine. They will only put Elon Musk or Warren Buffet there - their billions are enough to calm the population down.

But someone is above them - either he or she is the master of the world, or even the devil himself. They can also be aliens or entities from parallel worlds. This world is not real - the famous physicist and mathematician of today - Michio Kaku - has already said that. And it is also mentioned in the Koran, Buddhists meditate on it somewhere in their monasteries. Well, what will we talk about is a truth that gets tossed around all the time, but the power of hypnosis can turn almost anyone around place in this world.

And so little Maria runs to the employment office and stresses herself and everyone around that she didn't get her allowance - after all, she is a single mother - she is a parent. Well, yes, but little Maria doesn't realise that she chose her role before hers birth into this world.

She had already forgotten that she was a miserable grey spirit in the middle world - where she was trapped, either by her own fault or by a unlucky coincidence - and where she eagerly signed her soul to those huge devilish feathered lizards in the factory of artificial intelligence, and she signed the contract for exactly 79 years 2 months, two days, two hours, three minutes and some change to live on earth.

We are talking about earthly time, of course, which is clearly defined there by the ticking of the clock or by the ringing of church bells.

So, the monsters asked her "Do you want to be born a woman or a man?"

The desperate soul whispered "…and…what is this - a woman - what is a man,…I don't understand you…"

Well, those beasts of darkness began to explain all the pros and cons, benefits, roles in society, machine design - bodies, functionality, did not forget to mention the wonderful sensations of reproduction - sex, they made vague promises that she could be freed from the cycle of birth and death, once for all, but also they threatened,…they threatened hell, and last but not least they mentioned Paradise- i.e. the place where she would be happy for all endless ages.

Otherwise, they explained that on Earth - that is, in the place where she will be born - they have their agents, who control and test problematic people - anomalies. But then there are also a lot of other entities hanging around. Ghosts, aliens, beings from parallel universes and all sorts of other vermin. And everyone has their own agenda, their own interests. Of course, the greatest interest is in souls.

So they told her to watch out for a certain Nathrengar - that's the man in black hat and black cloak. And he's hanging around there - in that immense cosmic hypnosis - messing around with his diplomatic briefcase and a kind of large book in black boards.

He is lurking there, luring souls to Hell. He offers riches, lands, glory - passion and love, and in exchange he only asks for a signature of blood - but beware - it's eternal. That means… well, there is simply no way out of Hell, or at least we don't know anyone who ever escaped from him. So beware. So the hapless spirit chose the option - *woman*, then her escorts - blue chameleons with red eyes - took her to a colossal machine and even though she suddenly started to resist and scream and sob they tossed her on the conveyor belt, where they had to strip her. And then she was speeding into the jaws of the metal-cyber beast. It was like being devoured by a crocodile in the murky green hot waters of the Nile. The guts of the slimy ravenous creature squeezed and crushed her until she found herself in a kind of cramped pod. Suddenly it was quiet, warm and cozy. As if she were floating in a dark snug cocoon. She saw patterns - something like mandalas - and a kind of soothing angelic voice to her spoke. Then, out of nowhere, she began to zoom through a kind of spiral, a tunnel, made of silver wires. Then she slid - like on a sled - through a kind of red tunnel until she burst out into this Our World - reborn once again.

***

Samuel felt a sudden tug on his leg, snapping him out of his reverie. He looked down and saw the fox had crawled into his tent and was now curled up at his feet, staring at him with slanted eyes. There was something eerie about those eyes. They reminded him of the mural he had seen in Chicago's Chinatown, depicting a princess who was rumoured to be cursed by an ancient evil.

He knew he had to find a way to get rid of the fox. But something about her eyes haunted him. They were slanted like the ones of the Chinese princess with the same piercing gaze who could shape-shift into a fox. Could she be the same one? Had she come to his aid or to his doom?

He shook his head and tried to focus on his mission. He had been hired by a gallery owner to find a rare gemstone called chrysoberyl, a beryllium aluminate with a golden-green hue. He needed to find enough of it to cut into a stone that would complete a necklace for a mysterious princess from a hidden kingdom. A necklace that was said to have magical powers.

But time was running out. Outside, the storm was raging. The rain pounded on the tent and the wind howled like a banshee. Lightning flashed across the sky, followed by deafening thunder that echoed through the hills of the Jeseniky region. Samuel felt a surge of adrenaline. He knew he had to act fast. He grabbed his backpack and flashlight and prepared to venture into the dark forest, where he hoped to find the elusive chrysoberyl.

But as he was about to unzip the tent, he felt the fox's teeth sink into his ankle. He screamed in pain and kicked the animal of him. The fox snarled and lunged at him again, but this time Samuel was ready. He swung his flashlight and hit the fox on the head, knocking it unconscious.

He was about to drift off when he heard them. Voices. Then a flash of light lit up the tent walls, casting eerie shadows of figures outside, followed by a loud boom of thunder. The voices grew closer and Sam clutched the knife harder. The tent flap was yanked open and a flashlight blinded him. He couldn't see who they were, these invaders.

"Hand over the cash!" one of them barked from behind the glare.

"And everything else you got, your ID, your watch, your gold, anything, or we'll blow your brains out!" another one chimed in.

Sam braced himself for a fight and scanned his surroundings for any possible escape routes.

He tried to sound as confident as he could. "Get lost, I'm calling the cops!"

A tattooed arm with a large axe swung into the tent. "Yeah right, you won't have time for that, buddy!" another voice taunted.

"Man, he's in trouble, this jerk, I'm gonna teach him a lesson…" a third voice sneered.

"Shut up and hurry up!" another one snapped.

✳ ✳ ✳

He realized with horror that there were more of them, as he saw the axe coming down in the hand of the thug outside. His Krav-Maga skills and the small knife in his hand wouldn't do much good here.

"Okay, okay, I give you American dollars and you leave, okay guys?" he said.

"We'll gut you like a fish, you bastard." The thugs outside laughed in the rain.

Samuel didn't understand them very well, his Czech was pretty poor. But he understood the tone well enough - the situation was critical - this couldn't end well. The rain poured harder and suddenly a thunderclap shook the sky behind Samuel and a flash turned the night into a brief inferno. That's what Sam thought at first, but then he realised that one of the goons had cut the tent fabric behind him. The guy with the axe was about to strike again, but something happened. He let out a scream and dropped the axe and flashlight on the tent floor.

Samuel saw a fox biting the thug's hand.

Then both thugs vanished from the tent - hand in paw with the wild beast.

"Shit, shit, it has rabies,…" one of the guys said in fear.

Samuel didn't waste any time, he grabbed the flashlight and the axe, and as he turned around, he saw the knife in the crook's hand and his murderous eyes. Sam - instinctively - swung his axe - and blood sprayed his face.

He then ran out of the tent and looked around, shining his flashlight everywhere.

A man was sitting on the ground in front of him, clutching his neck, which was spewing red liquid. Another guy was lying nearby, twitching oddly, and when Samuel illuminated him properly, he saw the crazed fox furiously chewing on his brain. The fox whined with delight and shuddered in ecstasy. Apocalypse in the middle of a storm that suddenly stopped as if by magic. There was silence.

Samuel stood there, in the middle of the woods, at night, with an axe in his hand, covered in the blood of those scumbags. He watched the fox and it watched him.

***

He was haunted by her eyes. They were slanted like the ones in the mural, the one that showed the Chinese princess who could turn into a fox. He had been tempted to kill her with his axe. But then he understood - she was a demon and an angel - she had given him a chance to live. He stretched his hand towards her, the fox gazed at him with her amber eyes and then disappeared into the night. "Thank you, Chinese princess," Samuel whispered and then cried at his own insanity. He had to get rid of those bodies. *But wait, maybe one was still clinging to life.* He turned to the guy on the ground - he was already coughing up blood and whimpering. Samuel crept behind him, honed the axe blade, and swung. The wind shrieked in the trees and spattered the rustling leaves with red blood. Somewhere far away, lightning split the sky and thunder boomed over this dark and damned land.

Samuel had to dig a huge hole for all the thugs to squeeze in, and he was soaked with sweat. Then he hauled the corpses there and covered them with damp earth. He then flattened the surface and hid it with leaves and branches and stones. Samuel had to laugh at his own detachment, because he thought - well, now let's get to work and go find the biggest Chrysoberyl in the world. As if nothing had happened, as if he hadn't just slaughtered three people, as if he was trying to wipe out the horror of the whole situation with a casual motion. He had never killed before - until now - and with the help of his protector - the fox. He felt sick and vomited and remembered how he loathed and immediately turned off a movie in which a cop or a detective gagged at the sight of a corpse. "*Darn cliché,*" he said to himself and changed the channel.

Now he understood, but he didn't vomit, no, he just craved for having a bottle of whiskey with him. So he only lit a cigarette and thought about what to do next. He especially couldn't risk any attention from the locals now, after everything that went down here. He wasn't even sure if he was right. But on the other hand, and Samuel took a long puff, on the other hand he didn't come here for nothing…

And that bizarre encounter with that stranger - here - in the middle of the woods - with Nathrengar…

Either he was some kind of nutcase, or he really was a child of hell.

Sam looked at his hand, which had already healed from the wound that Nathrengar gave him when he forced Samuel to enter the Book of Darkness with a blazing knife sign.

He decided. He had to finish it. At any cost. He was exhausted, wrecked, mentally crushed, but he had to tear the stone out of the mountain's heart.

***

First, he arranged everything in the dryness of the torn tent - a pile of cigars, hammers, lighter, drill, long drill bits, chisels, shovel, flashlight. Then he filled himself with dried beef, which he hastily made some strong black coffee to wash down. And then he had the last donut with apricot jam.

Then he rolled up the wet tent as well as he could, carefully scanning the surroundings to ensure he didn't leave any evidence behind - given what happened here and marched to the outcrop of the pegmatite vein. Just in time as the storm returned and the lightning bolts were now chasing each other rapidly - well, simply in short bursts. He drilled into the rock, which exhausted his strength, then crammed the charge into the hole. The cigar of the dynamite was short. He lit a cigarette and envisioned holding a beautiful greenish crystal in his hand. How it shimmers and radiates in the dark moonlight.

When he was ready, he pressed the cigarette butt to the cigar and waited for it to ignite. Then he sprinted to hide in the trench in the clearing between the forked trees.

There was just a flash - perfect timing as the dynamite explosion was concealed by a thunderclap. *Great,* Sam thought, and that was the last thing on his mind because he felt a sharp blow on his forehead.

Darkness.

Nothingness.

***

Samuel was floating in a kind of virtual space of a computer game. All around were red pipes with black antennas and round windows through which he could see some ghostly beings or maybe spirits flying at high speed through those pipes. He heard wails, screams, shrieks, howls - pure undiluted horror.

One of the transparent beings somehow miraculously managed to stop inside the pipe and pounded on the window in panic and pressed its face against it. Samuel noticed this and also noticed that the being was looking at him and there was unspeakable anguish and sorrow in that look.

Samuel was dismayed and in shock. Where was he?

He swam closer to the round window and saw that the unfortunate creatures were being pulled with enormous force into what looked like a gigantic steam boiler. Even inside the pipe, unbearably high temperatures prevailed, as the air was shimmering in there and some of the ghosts seemed to be on fire.

Samuel was already at the window watching the visibly terrified entity. It had a translucent body - otherwise quite human - but its face had no eyes, no nose, and no mouth…

Nevertheless, Samuel understood what the being was telling him. It communicated with him using telepathy.

"This is not a dream! This is real!" it said.

"What? I don't understand. What do you mean?" Sam asked.

"Help me Samuel. Please help me!" begged the spirit, which was already starting to burn in a kind of strange orange flame.

The ghost cried tears from non-existent eyes. But Samuel saw those eyes anyway. And those eyes were so beautiful and deep and sad. They were full of love, and Samuel felt that love, for it filled him, through and through, leaving a warm feeling and at the same time causing immense pain, like when two lovers part.

"But how can I help you? How? What can I do?" Samuel's throat tightened with grief.

The soul extended a yellow glowing hand to Samuel and Samuel touched the window as if he wanted to grab it and pull it out of that awful pipe.

"Bring me that stone…that gem…it has a green colour and magical power to protect me from hell itself…find it for me Samuel!" and with those words, with that plea the soul disappeared into the hot pipe - mercilessly sucked up by the monstrous steam boiler of truly monstrous galactic proportions.

Samuel desperately touched the hot glass until it sizzled and he yelped in surprise and his hand jerked away again. He felt an indescribable sadness, for he felt that he knew that soul well, from eternity…

Samuel tried to fly through the virtual space along the pipe, trying to catch a glimpse of that ethereal apparition in one of the windows, but the unfortunate soul vanished.

Finally he reached a huge tall iron black gate. And it began to open slowly with a menacing creaking, flames shot out from its depths and the air rippled with heat. Sam felt that he was losing consciousness, that his vision was blurred, dimmed, and that he couldn't breathe. His heart was pounding.

He glimpsed a figure in the fire, a black figure of some kind of monster with horns on its head. The monstrosity grew larger, stretched out a claw and said something like: "Al abuablu…" in a booming voice that echoed.

The fire burned and blinded Samuel, and the thunder of the voice pierced his ears.

✱ ✱ ✱

Samuel opened his eyes. He felt a sharp pain in his forehead and saw blood on the stones around him. He had fallen from the cliff and landed in a pile of rubble. He groaned and touched the lump on his head. His fingers came back bloody.

He was soaked to the bone by the heavy rain that poured down on him. He shivered from the cold and looked up at the cliff. He had been searching for a pegmatite outcrop near the roots of a giant oak tree, but now there was no sign of the tree or the outcrop. Just a heap of rocks.

He tried to stand up, but he was dizzy and nauseous. The world spun around him. He crawled to the nearest boulder and leaned against it. He shouted at the stones, "Where are you? Show yourself! Please!"

The sky flashed and thundered, one after another, like an enormous pendulum clock counting down his time. Bam! Bam!

Samuel didn't need a flashlight. The lightning illuminated the forest and the rocks like a flickering neon sign on a dark street. He was an obsessed geologist who had brought a hammer, a shovel, a pickaxe and a searchlight with him. He had spent months looking for the elusive chrysoberyl, a rare and precious gemstone.

He focused on one large boulder that looked promising. He grabbed his hammer and started pounding on it. He chipped away at it with his drill and tweezers. He saw something shiny inside and his heart raced. He dug, broke, pulled, untangled - and finally freed a large piece of stone from the boulder. He tried to pry it open, to wrench it apart - like an angry dentist who can't extract a stubborn tooth.

"Fucking shit! Damned fucking stone! Come on!" he cursed and threw the stone on the ground. He glared at the boulder with rage.

The thunder roared louder and closer. The rain intensified. Samuel shook his head in disgust. He was hungry, thirsty, tired and in pain. He needed a break.

He reached for his box of cigarettes - the last one - ah - he had to savour this one - the first and the last were always the best. Every smoker knew that - it was their collective wisdom.

Samuel chuckled and whispered to the stones under his feet, *"You know the difference between meditation and smoking? No? Well, let me tell you: you can't smoke while meditating, but you can meditate while smoking…haha."*

He lit his silver Zippo until it sizzled and inhaled the smoke deeply into his lungs. Then he opened the zip of his trousers and relieved himself. He sighed with relief and sprayed urine on the rocks.

Then there was a flash and Samuel noticed something…

He bent down to get a better look. He took out his flashlight and shone it on the stone he had thrown away. He gasped and his heart skipped a beat.

The rain stopped and timid birdsong filled the air. The thunder rumbled again and the wind blew.

Samuel couldn't believe his eyes. He picked up the stone and examined it closely. There was a large translucent greenish crystal in it, bigger than a golf ball. And next to it another crystal, and then another smaller one - all three embedded in pegmatite.

It rained again and thundered sharply.

Samuel stood there with the stone in his hand and smoked his cigarette.

He was exhausted but ecstatic.

He had done it - he had found the chrysoberyl!

He felt a surge of joy, so strong that he wanted to roar. He opened his mouth wide, his face twisted in ecstasy and his eyes shining with bliss, but the only sound he heard was the thunder that cracked the sky again and again, tearing apart the gloom of this mysterious and harsh land. Samuel looked like he was weeping, but no, those were just ordinary yet wondrous raindrops that slid down his cheeks. Samuel took out his phone from his pocket and snapped a selfie with the crystal in his hand. Then he turned and gazed at the valley below Marsikov.

Some windows were already lit up. The wind stirred the treetops and Samuel heard the familiar tune in his mind - a song.

He knew what was about to happen…

He caressed the crystal one last time.

***

Samuel was driving his car through the Chicago suburbs on a rainy night. Suddenly, he felt a jolt from behind and saw another car speeding away. His car crashed into a lamp post and came to a halt. Samuel was stunned for a moment, then he moved his car to the side. He sat in his wrecked car and looked at himself in the rear mirror. He saw another pair of eyes staring back at him from the darkness. It was her…

"This is it. The end of the road," she whispered.

"What's going to happen now?" he asked.

"You know what you have to do, right?" she answered with a question.

"Yeah, I suppose so…" Samuel said sadly.

"Then why are you hesitating?"

"I don't know, I just…" he muttered and reached for a gun in the glove box. He turned around and saw no one in the back seat. Only a stuffed orange tiger in the corner, holding a perfume bottle in its paws. Samuel aimed the gun at the tiger.

"Goodbye, baby!"

A silver squirrel crouches on the broken lamp-post and surveys the scene below. A mangled car lies on the side of the road. A man is motionless inside. The rain beats down relentlessly. The place is a ghost town. Grass pokes through the cracks off the street. The buildings are crumbling and hollow. They are built of dark red bricks that look like dried blood. Behind them, there are towering skyscrapers with broken windows. The only signs of life are the stray cats, the scrawny rats, and the silver squirrel. It's a dismal and desolate place. The man in the car unfastens his watch and flings it out of the window. It lands with a splash. A gunshot rips through the silence of this dark place. But only for a split second, just enough to startle the squirrel away. Smoke curls up from the barrel of the gun. The rain keeps pelting on the ground and the car. *And that's it, another breath taken, another soul liberated from the shackles of this world. But who knows, maybe we'll bump into each other again,…in the better circumstances…*

There's plenty of time.

God knows…

The man stepped out of the wrecked car, clutching the tiger, a perfume bottle, and a gun in his hand. He fired another shot and heard an animal squeak. Samuel aimed again and saw a rat dart out of the car. He shot again and this time he hit his target.

He walked slowly towards the old warehouse made of dark red bricks. It was deserted and decaying. On the wall, there was a large mural painting - the painting from his childhood - with The Monkey King, the magician, the warrior, and the Chinese Princess. He stopped there for a while and gazed into the angel's eyes. Her eyes were like exotic crescents that seduced him with their wicked allure. Samuel felt himself drown in their dark depths.With a loud creak, he pushed the massive iron door open and shattered the eerie silence.

Samuel stepped into the dimly lit warehouse, where rows of wooden crates lay forgotten for decades. They bore labels and stamps from distant exotic lands he had never seen. He wandered among them, looking for the one he came for. Finally, he spotted it in a dark corner. A pyramid symbol with an "S" inside it was carved on the lid. He had found it at last. He darted his eyes around the room, looking for the one thing that could save him. There it was, in the far corner - a hefty pickaxe. He sprinted towards it and snatched it up. He swung it with all his strength at the wooden crate that concealed a black obsidian monolith. The crate splintered and the monolith emerged, gleaming in the dim light. He heard the sound of a helicopter approaching from above. "Shit!" he cursed. He had no time to waste. He felt his heart pounding in his chest. He ran his hands along the walls until he found a secret passage that was not visible at first glance. He glanced at the stuffed orange tiger and the perfume bottle. The bottle had the word "Eternity" on it. He set them down gently and reached into his pocket. He took out a piece of old newspaper and unwrapped it, revealing a stone with bright green crystals. He smiled, but his smile faded as he heard the sirens in the distance. He was running out of time.

Then a voice came from the door, speaking into a radio. "This is Mike Alpha X-Ray, I repeat Mike Alpha X-Ray, we have a suspect, send backup! He's armed!"

Samuel drew a knife and slashed the orange tiger open. A group of men in black stormed into the room, followed by a man in a hat and a long black cloak. Samuel turned around - their eyes locked - it was Nathrengar himself, posing as a detective - the mastermind behind everything.

Samuel yanked a rusty, oversized key from the tiger's mouth and a pistol from his pocket. He aimed the gun at the cops and fired wildly. With the other hand, he jammed the key into the monolith and twisted it desperately, but it wouldn't budge. The cops shot back from a safe distance. At last, the key clicked and turned itself - a narrow slit like a water slide opened in the monolith. Samuel dove in, dodging the bullets that pinged uselessly off the obsidian surface of the monolith, which mirrored his final glimpse of Nathrengar. His red eyes burned with rage.

"I will find you, Samuel!" Nathrengar roared.

"No, you won't, unless it's in hell, but I'm going somewhere else, where you can't go,..." Samuel sneered and snatched a bottle of perfume before the gate closed.

And then he vanished forever into the black obsidian monolith.

Nathrengar stood there and furiously pulled out a black book of Darkness and Fire. He flipped through and tore out a page with Samuel Greene's name and signature on it. He shredded it, crumpled it and tossed it aside.

Then he turned and said: "I will find you even if I have to become a saint!"

Then he bit into an apple he pulled out of his pocket. His phone rang…

He fished it out of the other pocket and answered the call with a flick of a devil claw.

"Yes, Mr. Dungwu, yes I understand,…" Nathrengar muttered.

He snapped the phone shut and barked at the cops. "The event - Mike Alfa X-Ray - is off, we have another intruder in Chinatown! And watch out - he can alter the reality. Head to Wentworth Avenue - restaurant - Seven Treasures!"

***

Samuel zoomed down the slide and laughed and shrieked like he did in his old childhood days when all that mattered was the present moment. And ahead of him was a clear, pure, endless horizon. He went so fast that he couldn't even breathe and then he just went faster and faster until his eyes flickered. Then he saw patterns like mandalas, shifting crystals in a kaleidoscope. It seemed like it would never end, but when Sam started to vibrate like a guitar string and his body stretched like a cooked noodle, he flew out from the other side of the intergalactic water slide and landed on the grass in the apricot orchard in the sunny valley and heard birdsong and classical music.

Samuel got up, brushed his pants and fixed his white wig, and reached into his pocket to pull out a bottle of perfume - just in time, for a carriage was already coming from afar. A beautiful carriage pulled by white horses. Samuel quickly sprayed himself with

"Eternity 8" brand perfume and hid the bottle behind his back. He waved at the carriage and the door opened.

"Hugo!" came the soft, heavenly voice of the girl. Then she leaned out of the carriage door.

Sara, his Sara!

She sang in lilting French "Monsieur Hugo, did you come back to us from far away to honour us?"

"And where did our penniless prince wander this time?" she added.

Hugo aka Samuel Green took off a tricorn hat adorned with a peacock feather "Good morning, princess, eh…I mean countess Sara, how you look today absolutely stunning."

"Only today?" the countess arched a brow playfully.

"Of course, you are my sun of suns and star of stars - the most beautiful in the universe, countess," Hugo praised the girl with long, sweeping black hair.

Her eyes were black and sparkled beautifully in the morning sun. They were full of the vitality of youth, and her lovely hands made her so charmingly expressive and affectionate. Hugo just stood there bowing until the countess couldn't help but laugh. She tilted her head with a smile and whispered in a melodious voice: "Now get in and don't keep us waiting - buyers will come today - from faraway Byzantium."

They sat opposite each other and gazed into each other's eyes as the carriage flew through the valley. The coachman whipped the horse to speed up. Hugo grabbed Sara's hand and slipped something into her palm. Sara opened it and gasped in surprise.

"Is this what I think it is?"

"Hmm,…" Hugo nodded his head and winked.

"Well, maybe now I can marry one of those wealthy suitors,…thank you very much, prince Hugo," she said gravely and a little sadly.

Hugo frowned "Sara, you know how much I love you,… that I would do anything to…"

Sara leaned towards Hugo "Shut up, you idiot." and she kissed his lips.

With her hand, Sara then drew the curtain of the carriage, which was already slowly nearing the castle on the hills above the valley.

***

Hugo stood on the terrace with a glass of wine, watching the girls splash by the fountain. He sipped and smiled, his heart pounding. Carriages rolled into the yard.

"The merchants are here, they have arrived," the sonorous voice boomed.

"Hugo!" came a sudden voice from behind.

His heart skipped a beat.

"I want you to meet our new chamberlain…"

Hugo turned and saw Sara walking onto the terrace with a man. Sara grinned and the man bowed.

"Please meet Mr. Boblig,…" she said with tinkling angel's voice.

Hugo tried to breathe, but something squeezed his lungs.

And when their eyes met, when he saw his face, Hugo knew right away who Mr. Boblig was…

The orchestra down in the hall started to play festive fanfares in honour of the guests.

Mr. Boblig sneered evilly, took his hat off and bowed without looking away from the petrified man.

"Ready to serve, your highness," whispered ominously their new chamberlain and the unfortunate prince could notice a small chuckle in the air.

A moment ago the world was so lovely, but the paradise was invaded by the chamberlain…

Hugo sensed this summer would be quite scorching…

But he kept his cool, because he knew already, that even the best looking apple can have the baddest taste…

He gave Mr. Boblig an ambiguous smile and winked "Welcome to the world of saints!"

Sara and Hugo, lovers true and dear
They roam through time and place
They seek for joy and peace to cheer
And they defy the devil and his grace

In every peril they do face a threat
But with their love they conquer all distress
They free each other from the foe's net
And they elude their enemies with finesse

Sara doth love Hugo with all her heart
And Hugo doth love Sara with all his soul
They never play each other false in part
And they fear none in their brave role

Sara and Hugo, a tale of love so fair
That speaks of truth and faith
It teaches us that love is a power rare
That vanquishes the ill and spreads the good in earth

The fool doth think he is wise, but the wise man knows himself to be a fool.

William Shakespeare ("As You Like It")

OMAR ZAHID (1973 in Havirov)

Omar Zahid is a versatile and adventurous writer, film director and entrepreneur. He has written four books, including his latest novel *Seven Treasures*, and directed three films that received international recognition. He has also explored various fields of business, such as music video production, talent representation, gemstone trading, IT development, content management and multilingual interpreting. He currently runs his company in Brno, Czech Republic and Chicago, USA, while also working as a remote interpreter for the UK public sector. Omar has a background in film and screenwriting from Belfast, UK, where he also volunteered for a local television station. He has lived in many different places around the world and once drove from Slovakia to Morocco in his old Honda Accord. Omar's stories are inspired by his own experiences and reflect the reality of life as he sees it. He is now working on his next thriller film Switcher Strikes, which is based on one of his previous books. By buying this book, you will join him on his exciting journey of creativity and discovery.

www.ingramcontent.com/pod-product-compliance
Lightning Source LLC
Chambersburg PA
CBHW021943101025
33863CB00051B/1315